Southwestern Book Trails

Photograph by John P. Schaefer

Lawrence Clark Powell

BRERETON

# *Southwestern Book Trails*

## *A Reader's Guide to the Heartland of New Mexico & Arizona*

LAWRENCE CLARK POWELL

William Gannon
Santa Fe, New Mexico
1982

This WILLIAM GANNON edition, published in 1982, is an unabridged reprint of the edition published by Horn and Wallace in 1963.

Reprinted by special arrangement with Lawrence Clark Powell.

| | |
|---|---|
| paperbound edition | ISBN 0-88307-656-X |
| clothbound edition | ISBN 0-88307-657-8 |

Library of Congress Catalog Card Number 82-082399

Address all orders and inquiries to:

William Gannon, Publisher
143 Sombrio Drive
Santa Fe, New Mexico 87501

*To Erna Fergusson and Patricia Paylore*
*Native Daughters of New Mexico*

# *Contents*

# *Preface*

IN A LIFETIME of trailing books in the Southwest, I have not spent much time searching for those I did not intend to read. The reading instinct in me is stronger than the collecting instinct, and this book is for readers rather than collectors. As much as I admire the work of the collector who preserves ephemera from oblivion, I am not at ease in the presence of such a person who has neither read his books nor is drawn to the region they describe. Such was my experience once in the private library of a man who had amassed a great collection of Southern California imprints, all in beautiful copies, mostly untouched by hands and eyes. Not only had he not read the books, he had never been in Southern California and never intended to go. Here was work of the mind, not the heart. There is no danger of my hurting his feelings; if he should buy this book, he won't read it.

It is not a bibliography or a collection of essays, such as my earlier books on the Southwest, although it partakes of both forms. In describing a few books from among thousands about the region, which I either own or have read in library copies, I shall pay no attention to points of issue, states of bindings, or other bibliographical niceties. I shall seek instead to relate books I have read to their settings which I have seen. I like books with a feeling for language as well as for landscape, books with those qualities which unite to form style: perception, emotion, precision—style, that fusion of the elements of individual character which results in the distinction of a writer and his work, which makes the difference between literature and journalism.

My Southwestern book trails are ones I have followed because of my own interests. I like history and travel, personal accounts, the arts and archaeology, creative fiction. I do not like books about frontier scum, about badmen, gunfights, feuds, hangings, ad bloody infinitum. Don't look for Billy the Kid or Tombstone or Wyatt Earp in *this* book. Nor do I write about cowboys and the range; after Dobie, I find there's nothing more to say. Although I recognize the role of economics and politics in shaping a new Southwest, I am not competent to write about either, other than to deplore many of their inevitable manifestations.

This is a good place to reiterate my debt to J. Frank Dobie, that great good Texan I have called "Mister Southwest." His *Guide to Life and Literature of the Southwest* changed my life when I read it in 1953, a change I have described in an essay called "Through the Burning Glass." Before Dobie I had written about the Southwest in a vicarious, academic way. A.D. in my life means After Dobie. He taught me newly to appreciate personal experience and perspective in my appraisal of books. Across two states I pilgrimaged, beyond the Pecos and the musically named rivers of Texas, clear to the banks of Waller Creek in Austin, where I visited Dobie and received his bibliographical blessing.

"If I were to do it over," he said, "I would write more about fewer books. Anyone can rustle up a plain bibliography. What's needed is the spotlighting of the few best books on a subject or a region. I won't do it over. If you do it, do it this latter way. Pick the few and then light them up with everything you've got."

This I have tried to do.

For ten years I have been ranging the Southwest, looking and listening, lecturing and listening to lectures, making friends in Texas, New Mexico and Arizona, going the highways and byways; and always reading, reading, going with books in my baggage, fusing life and literature, landscape and writers' love for it, blessed with the new vision Dobie gave me. A rich life but not a pioneering life; for, as I once wrote, I prefer a mattress to a sleeping bag, and I like my coffee out of china not tin.

This then is a book about books about places and people, and a book about places and people. It was written from my own direct experience of life and literature. As well as pleasing me in the writing, it is meant to encourage others to become travelling readers, reading travellers, to experience life with the heightened responses that literature produces in the sensitive reader.

"The impact of historical landscape," wrote Patricia Paylore, "can drive a man to books, to deepen his understanding and sharpen his insight, for to live on the surface, without concern for the roots that distinguish his little piece of history from any and all others, is to live shallowly, unknowingly, is to deny the sense of the past which sets us apart from less rational creatures."

At the end of each chapter I list the books and articles written about, so that the reader may identify and seek them out in library and bookstore, preferably the latter. Form your own Southwestern library, I say; never has it been easier and cheaper to do, as publishers and booksellers produce and distribute more and more on the region. The paperback revolution has brought many classics back in print for the benefit of the impecunious reader. My closing chapter is on printers and publishers, bookstores and libraries, specialists in Southwestern literature, and on regional bibliographies and periodicals.

It remains to thank those who have helped me—and promptly to add that fully to do so would require a biographical supplement to this book. Throughout the Southwest are kind friends who have helped me on my way and in my work. They will know how grateful I am. Two sources of strength must be acknowledged, however; the first is my employer, the University of California at Los Angeles, which has given me a rich livelihood; the second is my wife, Fay, who has made a loving home for me to return to from more field trips than can ever be counted.

L. C. P.

*School of Library Service*
*University of California at Los Angeles*
*June 1963*

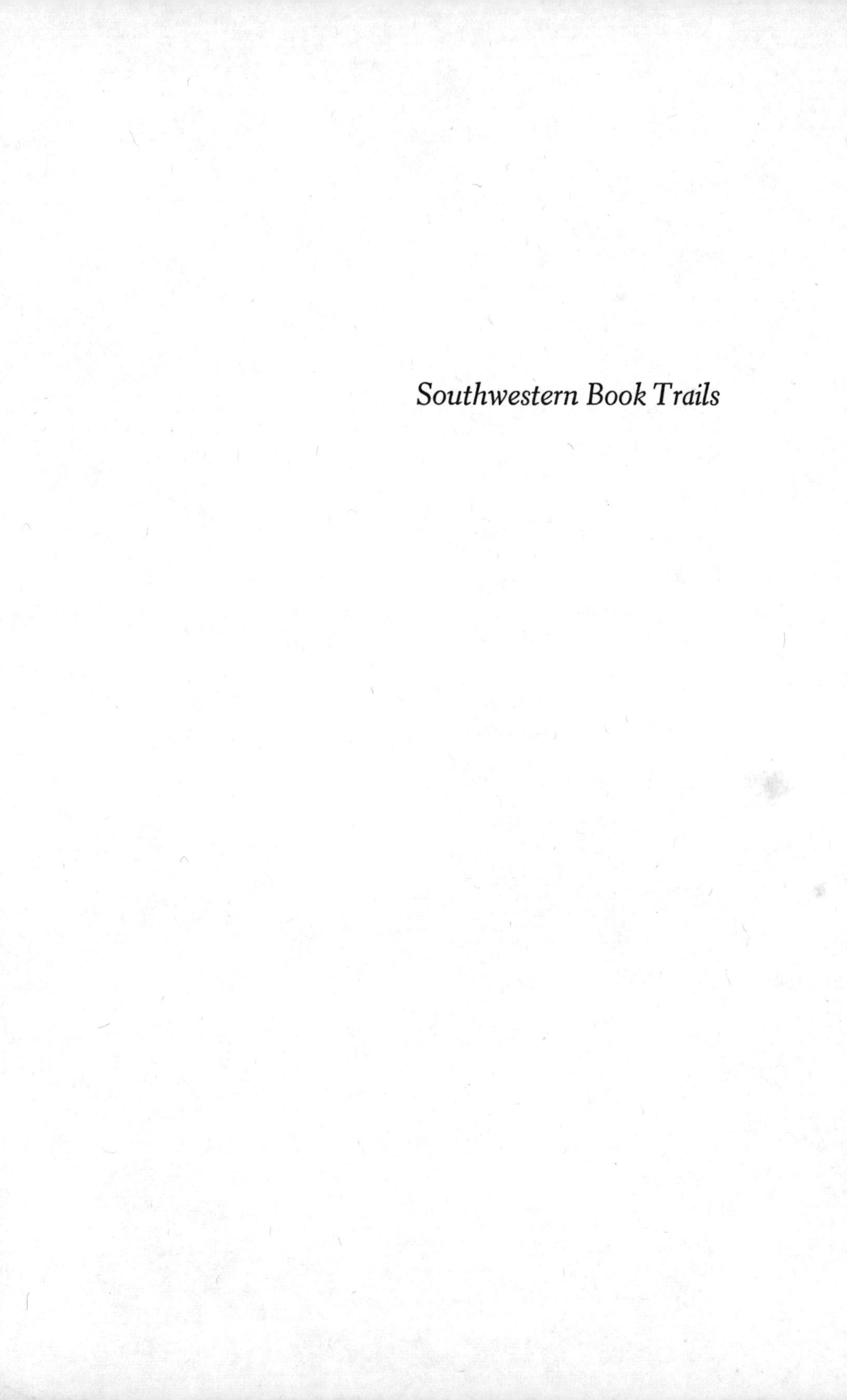

*Southwestern Book Trails*

# i. The Southwest

YOUR DEFINITION of the Southwest will depend upon who you are and where you are from. In his *Guide,* Dobie concentrates on the easternmost Southwest, beginning with his native brush country of south-central Texas, then heading west across the Rio Pecos and the Rio Grande, making a dry march down the Gila, and disappearing into the desert sands beyond the Colorado. Over the mountains lies Southern California which, in climate and Spanish origins, has much in common with the rest of the Southwest; and yet because of the industrialized urbanization it has experienced in the past generation, resulting in destruction of the natural environment, it requires consideration as a separate region; and I plan to supply a reader's guide to it. Dobie excludes it from his Southwest, as do most "eastern" Southwesterners.

The letterhead of the Oklahoma City Chamber of Commerce proclaims that place to be "The Heart of the Greater Southwest." On the contrary, W. W. Robinson, the Southern California historian, declares that Los Angeles is the magnetic heart of the Southwest, although located on the far western side of the body, in that it tends to draw everything and everyone to it. Economics determines, Robinson says; money is power and power produces culture. Was not Dobie drawn to the Huntington Library in San Marino by a fellowship and while there, did he not write his finest Southwestern book, *The Mustangs?*

The late Walter S. Campbell, the Oklahoma historian who usually wrote under the pseudonym of Stanley Vestal, compiled a bibliography called *The Booklover's Southwest,* from which he incredibly excluded Arizona. Texas-born Ed Ainsworth, veteran *Los Angeles Times* columnist, resolved his ambivalence toward the region by saying that his Southwest is wherever the mesquite grows. To which I replied that this would eliminate the Upper Sonoran and Transition life zones of northern Arizona and New Mexico, and include Kew Gardens, London.

"No matter what the historian or geographer or anyone else says it is or it isn't," I wrote in the preface to *Books West Southwest,* "the Southwest is recognizable upon sight, particularly from the air. Coloration is one thing, whether it be the dove-colored desert at Tucson and El Paso, the dark cedar-covered mesas of Coconino County, or the incarnadined Monument Valley; the sharp configuration of its landscape is another, from Cuyamaca and Baboquivari to the Sacred Peaks of San Francisco, Taylor, and Shiprock; or the absence of lush growth due to sparse rainfall, and the comparatively scant flow of its rios and arroyos secos."

Where do I take my stand when I survey the Southwest? Not in coastal Malibu where I live, nor in Los Angeles where I work; both are marginal vantage points, as were Dobie's in Austin, Campbell's in Norman. It is at the heart that I take my stand; at the heart of hearts, the *cor cordium,* in Albuquerque, New Mexico, that ancient crossing on the Rio Grande. I will be even more precise and say just where it would be in Albuquerque: on the station platform of the Alvarado, one of the last of the Harvey Houses and the most beautiful of them all, old gray stucco with the turquoise trim, its cool courts and shady patios inviting siesta, its Indian museum packed with old Pueblo artifacts, its slow heartbeat the coming and going of the Santa Fe trains.

There have I taken my ease over morning coffee, as the westbound *Chief* stopped for passengers and servicing, and I have lamented the passing of the named Pullman cars, the disappearance of some old favorites, Coconino Princess, Regal Junction, Pine Meadow, Red River Valley; and as I ruminated in that sweet early hour, I let my mind roam the region I call my Southwest, down river to El Paso, home-town of Tom Lea and Carl Hertzog and C. L. Sonnichsen, up river to Santa Fe and Taos, Alamosa and the Mesa Verde, to Las Vegas and Raton; or west on 66 through Arizona to Ash Fork and across the greatest western river of them all, to the desert and the mountains which wall off Southern California.

Albuquerque is the midway point, roughly equidistant between Fort Worth and Los Angeles, between Taos and El Paso, in the heart of the Indian country between Pueblo and Plains peoples, Spanish in origin and still bi-cultural, now molded by space-age developments; proliferating city on the river at the edge of the great plains, guarded by the Sandia range, a melting pot of the Southwestern elements which distinguish the literature I write about.

There in Albuquerque was born, raised, and still lives the best of all interpreters of this heartland, whose book *Our Southwest,* though published as long ago as 1940, before the great post-war changes in the region, is still the best introduction to the region. She is Erna Fergusson, the one I have called New Mexico's First Lady of Letters. Her book's distinction derives from her knowledge and sympathy which encompass the whole region of the Southwest: its geography, history, ethnology, agriculture, commerce, and arts. The region's total ambiance is present therein more than in any other book.

Erna Fergusson's Southwest ranges from the Staked Plains of Amarillo to Fort Worth and San Antonio—Dobie's Texas—west to Yuma and the River, with the heartland of Arizona and New Mexico in between. She writes of what she knows from travel and discovery, illuminated by reading and study. She writes of people she knows, of Indians, Spanish, and Anglos, of books she has read and understood, of ceremonials she has witnessed, of art she has responded to; and it is this personal quality, as distinct from academic research, that gives her book its lasting value.

Hers is not the *New Yorker*-style reportage, not the kind of cerebral job Edmund Wilson did on the Zuñi ceremonials. Her prose is of heart's blood, as well as of mind's ink. *Our Southwest* is out of date now by a quarter century, and does not cover the population explosion that has rocked Albuquerque, El Paso, Phoenix, and Tucson, or the effects of atomic bomb activity on the economy of New Mexico, or of electronics and bombing ranges on the Arizona deserts. What is timeless in Miss Fergusson's book is its probing of origins, its feeling for people and history, for landscape and weather. It is the best background book on the region, the best point of departure and return.

Erna Fergusson has also written a good volume about her native state, although *New Mexico, a Pageant of Three Peoples* too is out of date on the changes in the state's economy. A revised, updated edition is in press.

Basic also are the W.P.A. Writers' Program Guides to New Mexico and Arizona, first published in 1940 and inadequately brought up to date in facts and figures and illustrations by Joseph Miller. They are indispensable to the reader and traveller. I carry them on the seat beside me, along with road maps, when I am wandering the Southwest. A useful pictorial reference book is *The American Southwest* in the Golden Books series, an example of what can be done in the production of inexpensive books by color lithography.

In the American Folkways series of the 1930's and 1940's, two Southwestern volumes were published: Edwin Corle's *Desert Country,* on the Mojave and Colorado deserts of southeastern California, a region Corle was deeply attached to; and Haniel Long's *Piñon Country,* the Upper Sonoran zone of northern Arizona and New Mexico. Neither has the wide-lens vision of Erna Fergusson, neither has achieved the sophistication of *Our Southwest.*

Other comprehensive efforts to capture parts of the region are in *This is New Mexico,* a collection of articles from the *New Mexico Magazine,* edited by George Fitzpatrick, first published in 1948 and enlarged in 1962; and in *Arizona, its People and Resources,* edited by Jack L. Cross, an encyclopedic survey of the present state of the commonwealth, with articles by different writers on its history, commerce, agriculture, education and the arts.

A recent effort to present a rounded account of the region is W. Eugene Hollon's *The Southwest, Old and New.* It is stronger on the old than it is on the new. Written by an Oklahoma professor, influenced by Texan Walter Prescott Webb's classic *The Great Plains,* this work is plains-oriented and excellent thereon; but as it goes west it loses its grip and, for instance, ignores the interstate struggle for the water of the Colorado River, one of the supreme Southwestern facts of life. Hollon's accounts of contemporary Arizona and New Mexico are based on political newspaper reporting, and his treatment of the economic-political forces in the two states ably fills in the two decades since Erna Fergusson left off. It is in his survey of arts and letters, however, that Hollon is both superficial and inaccurate.

"The arid Southwest has always been too strong, too indomitable for most people," Erna Fergusson wrote. "Those who can stand it have had to learn that man does not modify this country; it transforms him, deeply."

Now let us look for evidences of this in some books about the Southwest.

## READING LIST

Edwin Corle. *Desert Country*. New York, Duell, Sloan and Pearce, 1941.

Jack L. Cross, *ed. Arizona, Its People and Resources*. Tucson, University of Arizona Press, 1960.

J. Frank Dobie. *Guide to Life and Literature of the Southwest*. Rev. and enl. Dallas, Southern Methodist University Press, 1952.

J. Frank Dobie. *The Mustangs*. Boston, Little, Brown, 1952.

Natt N. Dodge and Herbert S. Zim. *The American Southwest: A Guide to the Wide Open Spaces*. New York, Simon and Schuster, 1955.

Erna Fergusson. *New Mexico, A Pageant of Three Peoples*. New York, Knopf, 1951.

Erna Fergusson. *Our Southwest*. New York, Knopf, 1940.

George Fitzpatrick, *ed. This is New Mexico*. Albuquerque, Horn and Wallace, 1962.

W. Eugene Hollon. *The Southwest: Old and New*. New York, Knopf, 1961.

Haniel Long. *Piñon Country*. New York, Duell, Sloan and Pearce, 1941.

Lawrence Clark Powell. *Books West Southwest*. Los Angeles, Ward Ritchie Press, 1957.

Lawrence Clark Powell. "First Lady of Letters," in *New Mexico Magazine*, March 1962, pp. 22-23, 37-39.

Writers' Program, Arizona. *Arizona, the Grand Canyon State: A State Guide*. Completely rev. by Joseph Miller. New York, Hastings House, 1956.

Writers' Program, New Mexico. *New Mexico, A Guide to the Colorful State*. New and rev. ed. by Joseph Miller. New York, Hastings House, 1962.

## ii. *The Great Trailmakers*

THE FIRST BOLD ATTEMPT at a history of the Southwest, at least of the New Mexico–Arizona heartland, was by Hubert Howe Bancroft whose thirty-nine volume *Works* on the West range from Alaska to South America. In 1888 his *History of Arizona and New Mexico* drew on the original archives in Santa Fe before they were dispersed; this solid volume is packed to the margins with data, good for reference if not for reading.

In 1961 Horn and Wallace brought off a brilliant coup with a facsimile reprint of Bancroft, to which they persuaded the politically opposed senators of the two states, Democrat Clinton P. Anderson of New Mexico and Republican Barry Goldwater of Arizona, to contribute complementary and peaceful forewords.

As readable as Bancroft is not is Paul Wellman's *Glory, God, and Gold,* a history of the Southwest which is strong on the first Spanish-French explorers from Florida West and on the later fate of the Southwestern Indians. Its virtues are Wellman's ability to write narrative prose and his humanitarian view of the Indian minority. He makes no attempt to interpret the Southwest today.

I have mentioned Webb's *The Great Plains.* Valuable also as orientation reading is Frederick Jackson Turner's equally seminal, oft-reprinted essay "The Significance of the Frontier in American History." Henry Nash Smith's *Virgin Land; the American West as*

*Symbol and Myth,* is another philosophical history of the westward movement basic to an understanding of the forces that have shaped the region.

The greatest of all the western historians, however, is the one to whom I shall devote most of this chapter, one who went back to the beginning of the trails and followed them in the fullest sense, on foot and horse and by car, exploring the archives from Seville to Mexico City, and the land itself, every last weary mile the trailmakers first went. He was Herbert Eugene Bolton, out of Wisconsin, Texas, and finally California, where his career culminated in directorship of the Bancroft Library at Berkeley and, as Sather Professor of History, in his training of a whole generation of western scholars. Their tributes appear in *Greater America, Essays in Honor of Herbert Eugene Bolton,* a volume covering many aspects of western history.

Bolton was a big man, egocentric, flamboyant, aggressive, and hardy, a very bulldozer for work. His books on the great trailmakers, the conquistadors and missionaries, are fine and basic in our reading. To write them he unearthed, translated, interpreted, and understood the original sources, and then he went into the field and traced the routes, so that his writing has all the strength of rock bottom origins. If he had had more of a literary gift, more of a feeling for language and style, he would have become a western Gibbon, a Parkman, a Prescott. This was his only deficiency. Slight enough, among his virtues, the greatest of which was his disregard of the campus walls, his sense of reality, so often lacking in academics, which led him into a primary knowledge of the Southwestern lands whose configurations and climate were all determining in the way the trailmakers went and what they achieved.

First of the conquistadors was Francisco Vasquez de Coronado, who came from Mexico in 1540, taking a river trail north through Arizona thence eastward to the present site of Albuquerque and beyond to Taos, in search of the fabled Golden Cities of Cíbola. His finding them was one of the great disillusionments of history. They were none other than the adobe hamlets of the Pueblo Indians of Zuñi, crude, drab, even squalid mud dwellings, all of which have long since gone back to the muddy earth from which they were made. The descendants of these people seen by Coronado now live in the pueblo called Zuñi. Shell and turquoise ornaments they had, but there was no golden treasure such as Cortes had found in Mexico.

To write his *Coronado, Knight of Pueblos and Plains,* published in 1949, Bolton and two of his disciples, Hammond and Ewing, and others, went over Coronado's trail in what is now Texas, Oklahoma, Kansas, New Mexico and Arizona.

Coronado's advent into the Southwest was celebrated four hundred years later in New Mexico by the Coronado Cuarto Centennial Commission, an official government agency created to sponsor publications, ceremonies, etc., whose editor was Dr. George P. Hammond, Dean of the Graduate School of the University of New Mexico and later Bolton's successor as Director of the Bancroft Library.

Earlier in the sixteenth century another Spanish adventurer, Alvar Nuñez Cabeza de Vaca wandered across the continent after shipwreck on the Florida coast, accompanied by a dwindling band of survivors, taking eight years in all to reach the Gulf of California. His own story, and other epic accounts of early explorations, were edited by Bolton in *Spanish Explorations in the Southwest.* Vaca's narrative has been reprinted many times, most desirably in the Grabhorn Press edition.

Unfortunately Bolton never wrote a book on Cabeza de Vaca. *The Odyssey of Cabeza de Vaca* by Morris Bishop, longtime professor of Romance languages in Cornell University, versatile writer of light verse and mystery stories, is the best biography.

My favorite work on the sturdy wanderer is neither biography nor history. Whatever it is called, I find it one of the supreme creative achievements of Southwestern literature. Vaca's laconic narrative fired the imagination of Haniel Long, a professor of English from Harvard and Carnegie Tech who retired to Santa Fe in 1929 and lived there in constant literary activity until his death in 1956, founding the cooperative publishing venture called Writers' Editions. Long wrote a gloss on the Spanish explorer's report called *Interlinear to Cabeza de Vaca,* an interpretation of the man's character and the power that he found within himself. This little book has gone through several editions under its original title and later as *The Power Within Us,* and has been translated into French and German.

The figure who inspired Bolton's best biography was the Jesuit missionary explorer Father Eusebio Francisco Kino, a German who came to Mexico in the seventeenth century and founded the chain of missions in Sonora and what is now southern Arizona, the Pimería Alta. He had Cabeza de Vaca's stamina, and in addition he was a powerful organizer and propagator of the faith. *Rim of Christendom* is Bolton's biography of Kino, a major work on a major figure.

In 1961 Arizona celebrated the 250th anniversary of Kino's death with symposia and publications. To *Kino, a Commemoration,* Donald M. Powell contributed a bibliography, Ted de Grazia simple line drawings, and Patricia Paylore an assessment of Kino which is a masterpiece of Southwestern prose. She wrote:

"Many regions, perhaps all, have their heroes. Marquette and LaSalle, both contemporaries of Kino's, are honored in the areas of their activities. Salvatierra and Serra have a secure place in California. Pike and Fremont, Kearney and Carleton and Garcés and Oñate and a thousand others are figures of historical importance and significance for all time to come, and the continuing interpretations of their deeds and influence show no sign of diminishing.

"But there are fewer whose imprint was achieved creatively and positively, over a long period of time, in the same place, and of whom little but good can be said, no matter how scientific or factual the literary and historical approach. All men have their shortcomings, most heroes their weaknesses. It is only with a figure like Kino that we begin to approach the dedicated and single-minded giant whose beliefs and their translation into realities have changed the course of history and the face of the land. Kino was such a figure. To live in Pimería Alta two and a half centuries later is to prosper in a civilization which rests upon foundations he laid in the wilderness. Who else but a man of such intellectual and spiritual proportions and physical stamina could have created so much from so little?"

In California during the eighteenth century, the Franciscan father Junípero Serra founded a mission chain; in Arizona his fellow priest Francisco Garcés was equally renowned for his achievements. Garcés also left a diary. It was edited by Coues as *On the Trail of a Spanish Pioneer*—a heroic work, as is the novel based on it called *Dust on the King's Highway,* by Helen C. White.

The greatest of all Bolton's great works, however, was his discovery, assembling, and editing of the original diaries and documents of the Anza Expedition in 1778, the first overland trek from Sonora to California, a thousand colonists, baggage, and livestock, led by Captain Juan Bautista de Anza. This heroic migrator inspired Bolton to corresponding labors in archives and field. His preface to volume 3 of the five-volume set, published by the University of California Press in 1930, called "Retracing the Trail," is the high point of Southwestern scholarship.

Bolton's later editing of the Escalante diary, published as *Pageant in the Wilderness,* covering a journey in 1776 by Franciscans from Santa Fe to the Great Utah Desert and back, is an echo of the Anza, heroic in its own lesser way.

The labors of the New Mexican Franciscans do not compare with the Arizonans. There was none there to match Kino and Garcés. Willa Cather's novel about the nineteenth century Father Lamy, *Death Comes for the Archbishop,* probably the most esteemed of all Southwestern novels, is on a lesser scale, in a minor key, austere, strong, beautiful. In the novel, Miss Cather called Father Lamy, Latour. Paul Horgan's biography in progress of Lamy will be a triumphant work. His stories of New Mexican–Texan missionaries, *Humble Powers;* and the stories of Fray Angelico Chavez, a Franciscan priest of contemporary New Mexico, are chamber music after the organ strains of Kino and Garcés.

Before he left New Mexico to return to California, George P. Hammond continued as one of the founders of the Quivira Society, a publishing venture devoted to the reprinting of source works on the region. Its volumes are basic in a Southwestern library.

My favorite of Hammond's works is the massive set he collaborated on with Agapito Rey: *Oñate,* an editing and reprinting of the source documents of Juan de Oñate, the first colonizer of New Mexico, who came after Coronado to the capital at Santa Fe. Here is the raw material for creative literature.

A beautiful volume is *The Missions of New Mexico, 1776,* a description by Fray Francisco Atanasio Domínguez, with other contemporary documents. Translated and annotated by Eleanor B. Adams and Fray Angelico Chavez, with drawings by Horace T. Pierce, and published by the University of New Mexico Press in a bold design by Roland Dickey, its production was described by the designer in an article contributed to the *New Mexico Quarterly.*

Fremont's place as the Pathfinder had to be re-evaluated after the publication of *Stephen Watts Kearny, Soldier of the West,* a searching biography by Dwight L. Clarke, which for the first time established Kearny's stature as a western figure. As a topographical engineer with Kearny, James W. Abert wrote a comprehensive government report on New Mexico in 1846-47. This was reprinted in facsimile by Horn and Wallace, with a foreword by William A. Keleher. Clarke, a banker, and Keleher, a lawyer, exemplify the outstanding historical work on the Southwest being done by "amateurs."

I cannot close this chapter without mention of the avocational labor of love on the missions of Sonora and Arizona done by George B. Eckhart, whose vocation is that of Southern Pacific baggage-master in Tucson. Eckhart has established more facts, documented by his own photographs, on the Jesuit-Franciscan works of Kino and his successors than anyone since Bolton and another of his disciples, Father Peter M. Dunne.

"He has travelled the back roads of Sonora," wrote Patricia Paylore, "been stuck in her rivers, slept out under her stars, been lost, followed obscure leads, made friends with her people, located, photographed, made drawings of nearly every Sonora mission. And the inevitable concomitant is his serious study of books and documents that contribute in depth to his understanding and interpretation of what he has seen."

Now paved roads crisscross the Southwest and the speeding travellers who traverse them have no sense of the past. Save for occasional historical markers, there is nothing along the routes to remind them of the great trailmakers. Each city and town in the Southwest should erect fountain monuments to those who first came their way—conquistador, missionary, trapper, trader, evocations of Coronado, Kino, Smith, and Gregg as well as recognition of the power of water in the arid Southwest. These are our heroes, not the gun-toting riff-raff of today's TV.

## READING LIST

James W. Abert. *Abert's New Mexico Report, 1846-'47.* Albuquerque, Horn and Wallace, 1962.

Arizona Pioneers' Historical Society. *Kino; A Commemoration.* A Short Assessment by Patricia Paylore. Kino Sketches by Ted De Grazia. Bibliography by Donald M. Powell. Tucson, The Society, 1961.

Hubert Howe Bancroft. *History of Arizona and New Mexico, 1530-1888.* San Francisco, The History Co., 1889. (Another edition, Albuquerque, Horn and Wallace, 1962.)

Morris Bishop. *The Odyssey of Cabeza de Vaca.* New York, The Century Co., 1933.

Herbert Eugene Bolton. *Anza's California Expeditions.* 5 vols. Berkeley, University of California Press, 1930.

Herbert Eugene Bolton. *Coronado; Knight of Pueblos and Plains.* Albuquerque, University of New Mexico Press, 1949.

Herbert Eugene Bolton. *Rim of Christendom; a Biography of Eusebio Francisco Kino.* New York, Macmillan, 1936; New York, Russell and Russell, 1960.

Herbert Eugene Bolton, *ed. Spanish Exploration in the Southwest, 1542-1706.* New York, Scribner's Sons, 1916.

Willa Cather. *Death Comes for the Archbishop.* New York, Knopf, 1929.

Dwight L. Clarke. *Stephen Watts Kearny, Soldier of the West.* Norman, University of Oklahoma Press, 1961.

Roland F. Dickey. "Paging Procrustes," in *New Mexico Quarterly,* v. 26, no. 1, Spring 1956, pp. 58-74.

Francisco Atanasio Domínguez. *The Missions of New Mexico, 1776; a Description, with Other Contemporary Documents.* Tr. and annotated by Eleanor B. Adams and Angelico Chavez. Albuquerque, University of New Mexico Press, 1956.

George B. Eckhart. "A Guide to the History of the Missions of Sonora," in *Arizona and the West,* Summer, 1960 pp. 165-183.

Francisco Garcés. *On the Trail of a Spanish Pioneer, The Diary and Itinerary of Francis Garcés (Missionary Priest) in his Travels through Sonora, Arizona, and California, 1775-1776.* Tr. from an official contemporaneous copy of the original Spanish manuscript, and edited with copious notes, by Elliott Coues. 2 vols. New York, Francis P. Harper, 1900.

*Greater America; Esssays in Honor of Herbert Eugene Bolton.* Berkeley, University of California Press, 1945.

George P. Hammond and Agapito Rey. *Don Juan de Oñate, Colonizer of New Mexico, 1596-1628.* 2 vols. (Coronado Cuarto Centennial Publications, 1540-1940, v. 5-6). Albuquerque, University of New Mexico Press, 1953.

Paul Horgan. *Humble Powers.* Garden City, New York, Image Books, 1956.

Haniel Long. *Interlinear to Cabeza de Vaca; his Relation of the Journey from Florida to the Pacific, 1528-1536.* Santa Fe, New Mexico, Writers' Editions, 1936.

Haniel Long. *The Power Within Us; Cabeza de Vaca's Relation of his Journey from Florida to the Pacific, 1528-1536.* New York, Duell, Sloan and Pearce, 1944.

Alvar Núñez Cabeza de Vaca. *Relation that Alvar Núñez Cabeza de Vaca gave of what befel the Armament in the Indias Whither Pánphilo de Narváez went for governor (from the years 1527 to 1537) when with three comrades he returned and came to Sevilla.* Printed from the Buckingham Smith translation of 1871. San Francisco, Grabhorn Press, 1929.

Patricia Paylore. "The Testimony of Time," in *Arizoniana,* v. 1, no. 2, Summer 1960, pp. 7-10.

Henry Nash Smith. *Virgin Land: the American West as Symbol and Myth.* Cambridge, Harvard University Press, 1950; New York, Vintage Books, 1957.

Frederick Jackson Turner. *The Significance of the Frontier in American History.* El Paso, Texas, Printed at Texas Western College Press for Academic Reprints, 1960.

Silvestre Velez de Escalante. *Pageant in the Wilderness; the Story of the Escalante Expedition to the Interior Basin, 1776, including the Diary and Itinerary of Father Escalante.* Tr. and annotated by Herbert E. Bolton. Salt Lake City, Utah State Historical Society, 1950.

Walter Prescott Webb. *The Great Plains.* Boston, Ginn and Co., 1931.

Paul Wellman. *Glory, God, and Gold.* Garden City, New York, Doubleday, 1954.

Helen C. White. *Dust on the King's Highway.* New York, Macmillan, 1947.

## iii. River Trails

I SUPPOSE it is because I have lived most of my life in a land whose rivers—the Los Angeles, the San Gabriel, and the Santa Ana—have been made to lie down on concrete beds until they no longer bear any resemblance to natural water courses, that I am so obsessed by those Southwestern rivers that have proved more difficult to tame. Colorado, San Juan, Gila, Pecos, and Rio Grande—even the greatest of them, the Rio Colorado, is not much of a stream to look at by the end of summer, especially if one has been used to seeing the Hudson, the Ohio, the Missouri, and the Mississippi streaming the year round, high, wide, and handsome.

And so it is that I have had a passion for river courses in the Southwest, following them as high as possible to where they rise, descending them to where they empty out into other streams, seas, gulfs, oceans; at the same time collecting and reading and living with river books, until I now have a goodly shelf of them.

*Sky Determines,* declared Ross Calvin, and this I alter to read *Rivers Determine.*

Determine what? Merely the course of history, the economic and cultural development of the Southwest. The greatest metropolis of the West, a city destined inexorably to be the nation's largest, Nuestra Señora la Reina de los Angeles—good old L.A.—owes its life to the arterial flow of two distant rivers, the Owens and the Colorado. Four centuries of New Mexico's history in our time, and the pueblo culture of another five hundred years before, can be summed up in two short words: Rio Grande. In Arizona, the Salt River has made Phoenix, the Santa Cruz Tucson, while the Gila has been an immemorial lifeline of aboriginal culture, a trappers' and traders' trailway, and now a source of agricultural wealth; and yet all three of these streams are mostly subterranean.

Only in our time have the Southwest's rivers been controlled by dams, so that human works along their banks are not swept away each spring by the swollen flow of snow melt. The Roosevelt on the Salt, the Coolidge on the Gila, Red Bluff on the Pecos, Elephant Butte on the Rio Grande, Navajo on the San Juan; and the dams on the Colorado, beginning with the Laguna and the Imperial at Yuma, the Parker, rising to the Hoover, and now the Glen Canyon—these could be the subject of a great and thrilling book, a good dam book.

Let me start east and work west in this round-up of my favorite river-books; and go first clear to the easternmost of our Southwest to hail *Goodbye to a River,* John Graves's tribute to the Rio Brazos, that river of central Texas which he knew and loved as boy and man. When it was threatened by a dam with subjugation, he took his dog, bed roll, some grub and a book or two, and headed down river in a canoe, taking it in easy stages, and writing of the land and its lore on either bank, of history and local characters, as well as of each day's happenings. Graves succeeds in fusing past and present, history, geography, landscape and legend. His masters were Thoreau and Hemingway; a writer could do worse.

Every long river is many rivers. The Pecos, for instance, from its crystalline rise in the Sangre de Cristos of northern New Mexico to its dry wedding with the Rio Grande in Texas, suffers many changes. The upper river, the Pecos of the Sangres before it becomes a dry river, has been lyrically described by Harvey Fergusson in his book of memoirs called *Home in the West,* a twin-river book about the Rio Grande and the Pecos. Let me quote him:

"For more than two years, beginning when I was nine, I spent part of every summer on a ranch in the mountain country about the headwaters of the Pecos River. This region has a romantic beauty which made a great appeal to my young imagination. The lower slopes of the mountains are covered with virgin forests of yellow pine. They shoulder upward through dense jungles of spruce, to emerge above timber line in sharp spires of rock and snow. There are great green upland meadows, sprinkled with the pink and blue of wild cosmos, lupine and gentian, and groves of white-stemmed quaking aspen where the sunlight trembles among the restless leaves. The Pecos is a bright clear stream, running alternately through deep gorges of solid rock and open glades where blue spruce grows in isolated symmetry on perfect natural lawns. At its best, after the heavy rains of late summer, this country has an opulent beauty of its own."

One can descend the river from Cowles to Pecos village (and, if he is fortunate, as I once was, be halted there by the Corpus Christi procession crossing the road), cross the highway from Santa Fe to Las Vegas; and then follow the river from Ribera to Villanueva, edging irrigated fields and orchards, and finally see the river change and become the middle and lower Pecos, described by Dobie in the chapter "Trans Pecos" of his *A Vaquero of the Brush Country*:

"Up towards its head springs the color of the water is silver, and it runs shining and gay. Then about Roswell and on down to Carlsbad it becomes deep and blue. Lower down it takes on the color of red, and for hundreds of miles courses turgid and sullen. As it nears its union with the Rio Grande the waters borrow the grayish cast of the rocks that for a great stretch wall them in."

Last summer in the Taos Bookshop I found a pamphlet on the Pecos wilderness area, *Trail Guide to the Upper Pecos,* one of the series called *Scenic Trips to the Geologic Past,* published by the New Mexico Bureau of Mines. It is a gem of a booklet. The entire series of nearly a dozen items can be bought for less than five dollars from the New Mexico Institute of Mining and Technology at Socorro.

Few states are as fortunate as New Mexico in having both Erna and Harvey Fergusson for spokesmen. Like his sister, Harvey was born and raised in Albuquerque, and his *Home in the West* is the best of all Southwestern autobiographies of boyhood and youth. The mountains of northern New Mexico and the rivers which drain them are the lifeblood of Harvey's books, whether it be his history of the river valley called simply *Rio Grande* or his series of New Mexican novels beginning with *The Blood of the Conquerors* and *Wolf Song* and culminating in *Grant of Kingdom* and *The Conquest of Don Pedro*. His novels are at the pinnacle of Southwestern fiction, true to life and love and landscape, written with a feeling for language and no wasted words. Unlike Zane Grey, whose novels went from good to bad, Harvey Fergusson's have gone from good to better, have improved with each successive work, deepening, richening, mellowing. Although he left his native state fifteen years ago and now lives in Berkeley, Harvey Fergusson has never cut his New Mexico lifeline. Each succeeding book by Fergusson, though written *in absentia,* is more than ever deep New Mexican.

Although born in Buffalo, Paul Horgan came as a boy to Albuquerque, worked later as librarian and assistant to the president of the New Mexico Military Institute in Roswell, and has made the state his home, as a practitioner and patron of letters, art, and music. After a series of novels and stories, his work culminated in *Great River, the Rio Grande in North American History,* on which he labored for fourteen years and for which he received the Pulitzer Prize. It is the most ambitious and impressive of all Southwestern river books.

I had the good fortune of being in Albuquerque at the time it was published in the fall of 1954; and with Volume One on the seat beside me I played hooky from a conference and drove down the west bank of the river to Isleta, found a secluded spot in a golden grove of cottonwoods, opened the book and in one of those conjunctions of the time, the place, and the book, in which landscape and literature came into perfect register, I read these words about the trees which surrounded me:

"Its silver bark, its big, varnished leaves sparkling in the light of summer and making caverns of shade along the banks, its winter-hold of leaves the color of beaten thin gold lasting in gorgeous bounty until the new catkins of spring—all added grace to the pueblo world. The columnar trunks were used to make tall drums, hollowed out and resonant, with skins stretched over the open ends. The wood was hot fuel, fast-burning, leaving a pale rich ash of many uses. Even the catkins had personal use—eaten raw, they were a bitter delicacy in some towns. And in that arid land, any tree, much less a scattered few, or a bounteous grove, meant good things—water somewhere near, and shade, and shelter from the beating sun, and talk from trifling leaves."

I know the Rio Grande only in the first two of its three-state flow, not having followed it down stream from El Paso, through the Big Bend, along the Texas-Mexico border to its union with the Gulf of Mexico at Boca del Rio near Brownsville. My favored route is up-stream from Albuquerque, past the pueblos, through the gorge of the Taos plain, on into Colorado to Alamosa, and westward up the narrowing stream past Creede, toward its source in the San Juan range of the Rockies.

One of the uses of books about the land is to make our own vision clearer and more subtle; for instance, to see the pueblos with Horgan's eyes, as in this passage:

"The cities were much alike in form, varying most in color. The Rio Grande long ago cut down through different layers of buried color, revealing each at widely separated places along its course. The local soil made the walls, and gave them their color. The prevailing hue was pale, the Indian tan of dry river mud, wherever the pueblos sat on or near the river course in its most pastoral character. Where lava still showed in the soil in spite of centuries of weathering after forgotten upheavals, the earth, and the town, had a gray look, as at San Ildefonso. Up the Chama River, the ancient pueblo of Abiquiu had a dusty vermilion adobe, taken from the red hills and cliffs. A faint pink clay went into the pueblos of the Piros farther down the Rio Grande near Socorro."

Neither Horgan's nor Fergusson's is *the* companion book for such an ascent, or descent, but there is one that is—a photographic tour of the 1800-mile course of the Rio Grande del Norte from snow melt and brooklet to Gulf. *Rio Grande, River of Destiny* by Laura Gilpin of Santa Fe, one of the Southwest's creative photographers, is an ideal river guidebook.

Needed is a similar book on the San Juan, the Colorado's major tributary which rises just over the divide from the source of the Rio Grande, flows south and west past Pagosa Springs to Farmington and Shiprock, through the Goose Necks to its deep-walled confluence. High in Wolf Creek Pass I have seen the San Juan rise in a myriad seeping rivulets, have seen it born and grow to riverhood. In flow it is New Mexico's greatest river.

Although the Gila is mostly an Arizona river, it rises in New Mexico, high in the Mogollon wilderness once the stronghold of the Mimbres Apaches, the Red Willow people; and near its headwaters are prehistoric cliff dwellings accessible only by jeep. I have ascended the Gila along many miles of its far cross state flow, beginning at the sandy junction with the Colorado above Yuma, following its flat bed across the greasewooded desert floor to Gila Bend; then a gap in my travels before I joined it again at Winkelman, another junction point, with the San Pedro, southern Arizona's major stream; and then I have entered the gorge it has cut through the golden brown mountains after it leaves the lake in back of Coolidge Dam. I have lingered there on the dam, a mild day of early spring, looking out over water and earth through a blue veil, across the submerged lands of the San Carlos Apaches to the Mogollon Rim and the copper mines at Morenci and Santa Rita, seeing the Graham range snowbound and inaccessible in the southwest; while the pageant of history streamed by. No pueblo culture flourished on this stretch of the river; the Apaches ruled otherwise.

There are two books about the Gila which evoke this sense of the river's historic past: *River of the Sun* by Ross Calvin, and *The Gila* by Edwin Corle.

This brings us to the Colorado, a river too savage to be tamed by aboriginals and early settlers. Its course through the Southwest, after leaving its mountain origins in Colorado and Utah, is through deep canyons and deserts. The history and development of New Mexico and Arizona, so close on the map, so different in cultures, can be illuminated by a study of their major rivers. Garcés was the first to call it the Colorado, the first to descend to the Havasupai Falls and the oasis there, but he stayed not. The Indians of the lower reaches, the Mojaves, Cocomaricopas, and Yumas, never built a pueblo culture and were successful in rejecting the Spanish; in fact in 1789 they murdered Garcés and his fellow priests, soldiers and colonists who sought to settle at Yuma. Douglas Martin in *Yuma Crossing* has written the history of this wild point on a wild river.

Frank Waters in *The Colorado* has told the long river's story in prose of power and beauty. As neither Arizonan nor Californian but Coloradan, his chapter on the struggle for the river's flow is more impartial than anything out of Phoenix or Los Angeles.

There is a beautiful little novel about the river from Needles upstream to the deep canyons, a kind of Huck Finn of the Colorado, about a Mojave boy and a white boy who run away up river. *Crazy Weather* is by Charles L. McNichols, a former Indian agent, and it accounts in prose shorthand for the lack of anything but the most primitive culture along the heat-crazed, oft-flooded lower reaches. The "Great Colorado Novel," which will encompass the whole epic flow, is still to be written. Frank Waters could write it.

In spite of dams and modern boats, the river is still a wild one. Its power and beauty are revealed in a photographic record, similar to Laura Gilpin's of the Rio Grande. *Torrent in the Desert* by Weston and Jeanne Lee is a history of the river, illustrated from kodachromes of great beauty, all the way from the snowy sources of the Green and the Grand which unite to form the main stream, past the roll call of tributaries—the Gunnison, the Dolores, the San Juan, the Virgin, Little Colorado, and the Gila, thence to the estuary in the Gulf of California—Oñate's Mar del Sur, the Sea of Cortez.

These are the mainstreams whose roll I have called. The little rivers also call for books to be written about them. In New Mexico, the Red River—the Little Red, to distinguish it from the great tributary of the Mississippi—which rises in the lee of Wheeler Peak and makes a short run to reach the Rio Grande below Questa; the even shorter Arroyo Hondo which cuts across the Taos plain; the muddy Chama and the Jemez. In Arizona, the Little Colorado and the Bill Williams, north country streams; the White and the Black which form the Salt; the Verde and the Hassayampa; the Aravaipa and the San Pedro and the San Francisco which also swell the Gila; and the southernmost Santa Cruz which rises in the Santa Ritas, heads for Mexico, then reverses its course and forms the fertile valley between Nogales and Tucson, and ends up nowhere. All have determined local history; all call for chroniclers.

## READING LIST

Ross Calvin. *River of the Sun; Stories of the Storied Gila.* Albuquerque, University of New Mexico Press, 1946.

Edwin Corle. *The Gila, River of the Southwest.* New York, Rinehart and Co., 1951.

J. Frank Dobie. *A Vaquero of the Brush Country.* Boston, Little, Brown, 1929. (Another edition with a Preface by Lawrence Clark Powell, 1959.)

Harvey Fergusson. *The Blood of the Conquerors.* New York, Knopf, 1921.

Harvey Fergusson. *The Conquest of Don Pedro.* New York, Morrow, 1954.

Harvey Fergusson. *Grant of Kingdom.* New York, Morrow, 1950.

Harvey Fergusson. *Home in the West, an Inquiry into my Origins.* New York, Duell, Sloan, and Pearce, 1945.

Harvey Fergusson. *Wolf Song.* New York, Knopf, 1927.

Laura Gilpin. *Rio Grande, River of Destiny; an Interpretation of the River, the Land, and the People.* New York, Duell, Sloan, and Pearce, 1949.

John Graves. *Goodbye to a River.* New York, Knopf, 1960.

Paul Horgan. *Great River: The Rio Grande in North American History.* 2 vols. New York, Rinehart, 1954.

Weston and Jeanne Lee. *Torrent in the Desert.* Flagstaff, Arizona, The Northland Press, 1962.

Charles L. McNichols. *Crazy Weather.* New York, Macmillan, 1944.

Douglas D. Martin. *Yuma Crossing.* Albuquerque, University of New Mexico Press, 1954.

New Mexico Bureau of Mines and Mineral Resources. "Trail Guide to the Upper Pecos," no. 6 of the Bureau's series *Scientific Trips to the Geologic Past.* Socorro, New Mexico, 1960.

Frank Waters. *The Colorado.* New York, Rinehart, 1946.

# *iv. Indian Ways*

MY KNOWLEDGE of Southwestern Indians, except for the lands they inhabit and the artifacts they have made, is second-hand. I have never known any Indians personally, nor have I witnessed any of their ceremonials. I once helped the Acomans haul a *viga* to the roof of the church they were repairing, but no introductions were consummated, no polite phrases exchanged. I simply got on the rope with them and hauled away for dear life and St. Estevan. As a baby in my mother's arms on the station platform in Las Vegas, I was pacified, my mother wrote in her journal, by sight of the Indians selling pottery. I do not have the genius of a D. H. Lawrence which enabled that writer to perceive, absorb, and express essentials in a matter of minutes, hours, days, so that his essays, stories, and a novel about the Indians of the Southwest are marvelous things.

Nor can I say that I am attracted by Indian ways of life; they are mostly incomprehensible to me. I abhor cruelty; stoicism is alien to my nature; austerity has never appealed to me, although none of these qualities are characteristic of the Pueblo tribes. So this chapter will hardly be authoritative. Call it one man's impressions of Indian landscape and literature—literature about, not by Indians. Not knowing any Indian tongues, I can only point to the English translations by Washington Matthews and Father Berard Haile of Navajo chants and nightsongs, to the poetical versions of them by Mary Austin in *The American Rhythm,* to the English versions of Zuñi and other pueblo tales by Frank Hamilton Cushing and Frank Applegate, to the song magic of the Papagos, rendered by Ruth Underhill in *Singing for Power.*

Any literature beyond the primitive chant or tale is usually the product of leisure. The struggle for existence in an arid land, without benefit of labor-saving devices, has not afforded southwestern Indians leisure for literature. What art they have created in textiles, basketry, and ceramics, silver and turquoise, has been functional or ritualistic-ornamental. Thus the Hopi Don Talayesva's autobiography, *Sun Chief,* is nearly unique; and even then it was a recorded collaboration between him and a Yale anthropologist. He didn't sit down and write it. As Dobie remarks, it is one of the few accounts we have of an Indian's sex life, but it poses no sales threat to *Tropic of Cancer.* Simpler, beautiful in format, and written by himself, is George Webb's *A Pima Remembers,* a memoir of the Arizona Indians along the Salt and the Gila rivers, a peaceful tribe given to agriculture and badly treated by the whites of Phoenix and environs.

So what do I present as the literature of Indian ways? What do I choose from the literature totalling thousands of volumes written by whites *about* the Indians of the Southwest, only a fraction of which I have read? My answer is, a few such books as I have felt compelled to own in order to have available, books of fact, books of feeling, the products of mind and emotion.

Hodge's *Handbook* is the classic reference work on the Indians north of Mexico, and for all of North America, not merely the Southwest. It is one of the great works that came out of the springtime of American ethnology, out of bureaucratic Washington, inspired by the pioneer work of Bandelier and Cushing, begun by teamwork in the Bureau of Ethnology and brought to completion in 1910 by Frederick Webb Hodge, then in the prime of life, English-born, self-educated in field and library, a man who was to go on to fame as Director of the Heye Foundation in New York and of the Southwest Museum in Los Angeles, and live on to a serene and lucid old age. Hodge! I knew and loved his gentle ways during the final decades of his life, and learned from him, born teacher that he was.

In addition to the *Handbook,* I cherish his monograph on Hawíkuh, an account of his excavation of one of the lost cities of Cíbola, the pueblo to the west of Zuñi. It is a model "dig" book, printed by Ward Ritchie, with beautiful collotype plates of Zuñi country. Telulí, the Zuñis called Hodge, likening him to the prairie dog who digs his own cellar.

Hodge died at Santa Fe in 1956, and by dispensation of the United States Government he served so well, his ashes were scattered from a low-flying airplane over the site of Hawíkuh.

Another great "dig" was that by Alfred V. Kidder at Pecos Pueblo. His account of it appears in one of the volumes of the Peabody Museum at Harvard; and his final reflections are found in his *Introduction to Archaeology* and in a reminiscence he contributed to *The Kiva,* in which he recalled his earliest "dig," as a Harvard graduate student, together with Sylvester Griswold Morley and John Crowe Ransom, directed by Edgar Hewett, on the Mesa Verde. Here is a sample:

"The most impressive of the upper set of ruins was a square tower, placed on a corner of a ledge near the bottom of the canyon. Its walls rose straight up, course after course of trim, well-cut stones, to a height of over thirty feet. It was so small in cross-section, so slim and delicate looking that one wondered how it could have withstood the wear and tear of the centuries which must have elapsed since those hunted, peaceable masons were driven for refuge to places such as this."

The literature of the Mesa Verde, queen of the pueblos, now a National Park, abandoned in the twelfth century because of unbroken drought, is rich and varied, from Nordenskiold's monograph to the chapter, "Tom Outland's Story," in Willa Cather's novel *The Professor's House.* Frank McNitt's *Richard Wetherill: Anasazi* is a monograph on the discoverer of the Mesa Verde culture. Recall that in 1776 the Escalante expedition came within a few miles of the discovery. A fruitful and meaningful children's book is Conrad and Mary Buff's *Hah-nee of the Cliff Dwellers.*

See how I'm drawn away from the "facts" of Hodge's *Handbook* to the imaginative yet faithful recreation of the Indian past by the Buffs! And this is the delight of Southwestern book trails; they lead back and forth, in and out of fact and fiction, bringing all aspects of life together in one meaningful whole.

Edgar Hewett's *Ancient Life in the Southwest* is the best introduction to the archaeology-ethnology of the Indian peoples. The early chapters in Horgan's *Great River* are marvelous accounts of the river pueblos, whose culture was enriched by the thirsty ones who emigrated from the Mesa Verde.

The Spanish-Mexican-Anglo impact on the Indians is the subject of a recent comprehensive book by the Tucson anthropologist Edward Spicer called *Cycles of Conquest,* the best work of its kind.

Monographs on the individual tribes are found in the Civilization of the American Indian series published by the University of Oklahoma Press and now numbering more than sixty volumes. This is one of the major Southwestern projects of our time, conceived by Joseph Brandt and continued by Savoie Lottinville; if one has the shelf space, he should own the entire series. The *Navajo Year Books,* published by the tribal agency, are useful reference works. One of my favorite volumes on the Southwestern Indians is Alice Marriott's *These Are The People,* simply written, in fitting format by Merle Armitage.

It should not astonish my readers to learn that Erna Fergusson has written a book on the Indians fully as significant as her book on the region. *Dancing Gods* is an account of their ceremonials. Unlike her friend Paul Horgan, a devout Catholic who regards the Pueblos' religion as a preliminary to Christianity, Miss Fergusson writes of the Indians' religion as one of full realization for them.

"Suddenly I knew how alien I was in that Indian world." she writes. "It is a separate world. The white man sees it, he touches it, some even have the temerity to try to break into it, to change it. But they cannot. For this is a world apart, a brown world of brown people. They come out of their world sometimes to speak to us, for they understand our language; but when they withdraw into their world, we cannot follow. They live close to the earth. The mass for a pale god who died on a cross did not reach these people. They do not understand. A religion of an idea, of an ideal, is foreign to them. Their religion is of earth and the things of earth. I thought of all these brown people whom I had seen dancing their prayers, pounding them with their feet into the earth, which is their mother. Her ways are close to them, even when they are hurt. They understand the earth, they dance their prayers into the earth, and they pray for real things, for sun, and rain and corn. For growth—for life."

Frank Waters' *Masked Gods* is a more ambitious work on the Indians' religion, tending to mysticism. Waters has lived with and knows the Indians, from the river people to the Hopi pueblos. His novel, *The Man Who Killed the Deer,* is the classic account of the peyote cult and of the Indians' dilemma, transfixed between two cultures, belonging to neither.

The Penitente cult is the subject of Alice C. Henderson's *Brothers of Light,* a book to take with you to Mora, Trampas, and Peñasco, where the crosses for the procession may be seen stacked behind the churches; and reading it there, you may sense something sinister in the air, emanating from the cruel rites of the flagellants. It must be said, however, that this cult is Spanish Catholic, not Indian.

The Indian trader is a key figure in the Southwest of the past generations. Better roads and pickup trucks, enabling the Indians to go in and out of urban trading centers, and the passing of the home craftworks, meant the end of the trader. His rise, prime, and decline are the subject of Frank McNitt's *The Indian Trader.*

The popular belief is that fact and fiction are opposites, and I must admit that much of the fiction about the Southwest is only distantly related to fact. Fact alone, however, is rarely found in pure form. Examples are weather and temperature tables, population statistics, birth and death dates of people. Is Hodge's *Handbook* purely factual? No. It is an arrangement, an interpretation by several minds of factual data. Man selects, arranges, and passes experience through the filters of his heart and brain. My own work on the Southwest, based as faithfully as possible on "facts" I have seen, read about, and felt, has been inescapably colored by my own nature, by what it subconsciously accepts and rejects. The academic insistence upon objectivity is a vain desire. By his very choice of subjects to be objective about, a man reveals his own personal biases.

When I come now to write about Southwestern fiction of the Indians, it will be of a very few choices from among hundreds of novels, selected for the masterful way their authors have passed facts through the filters of their own thoughts, desires, and imagination, so as to illuminate experience, thus intensifying light and shadow and enabling us to see what they saw with their chromatic vision. This is the supreme creative gift, given to few writers, and which sets them apart from the hacks and the pulpers who produce a steady stream of "Westerns."

What Willa Cather eventually came to see, from her first passing glance at the bronze statue of Father Lamy that stands before the Cathedral in Santa Fe, is the novel *Death Comes for the Archbishop*. The same visionary transformation was experienced by Zane Grey, when he came west for the first time as dentist turned hunter, saw the colored canyon country of the "Arizona strip,'" and was moved thereby to create the novels of his prime: *The Heritage of the Desert, Riders of the Purple Sage, The Rainbow Trail,* and *The Light of Western Stars.*

From such novels as the Cather, the White and the Grays, the Waters, the McNichols, and others I have cited and will cite, one gets a full-dimensional view of the Southwest, of facts in meaningful arrangement and illumination, that can never be derived solely from reference books, histories, biographies, and encyclopedias.

There is no history of the Apache Indians, no biography of its chieftains, which tells us more truly or makes more impact upon our minds and hearts than the novel *Apache* by Will Levington Comfort, that transcendent last book he wrote, in which all his gifts coalesced, incandesced, and did not melt into romantic sentimentality. It is the lean and muscular story of Mangus Colorado, the greatest Apache of them all, leader of the Mimbreños, who was betrayed by the perfidious whites. Fiction? Yes; and Fact, also, the fusion of which produced Literature.

"It is authentic," Hodge told me. "Comfort did some of the research for it here in the Southwest Museum"; and he opened his desk and took out the original typescript of the novel, which Comfort had given to the museum before his death a year after *Apache* was published. He died in a hallucinatory state, his daughter Jane told me, believing he was Mangus and his son-in-law, seated at his bedside, was Cochise.

The finest novel about Cochise, chief of the Chiricahua Apaches, is Elliott Arnold's *Blood Brother,* also based on deep research, but with an added fictional love interest which diminishes the book's versimilitude.

Two novels of the Navajos I place among the finest fiction of the Southwest: *Laughing Boy* by Oliver La Farge and *People on the Earth* by Edwin Corle. In *Taos* Irwin Blacker wrote a powerful novel of the Pueblo Revolt of 1680 and the Spaniards' withdrawal down river to El Paso, the first in a projected trilogy of the Spanish occupation of New Mexico.

I have long been interested in the arc of a novelist's career—his take-off, ascent, apogee, descent, nadir. Sometimes, as in the case of Zane Grey, he attains zenith in his first books and everything subsequent is decline. Steinbeck rose slowly, reaching his peak in *The Grapes of Wrath* only after ten years of work. Hemingway shot up to *The Sun Also Rises* and *A Farewell to Arms,* then succumbed to success. Edwin Corle's first novel, *Fig Tree John,* portraying the conflict of an Indian and his son in the Coachella Valley, is his best novel, followed by one nearly as good—*People on the Earth.* Harvey Fergusson's early novel, *Wolf Song* and his latest novel *The Conquest of Don Pedro,* separated by thirty-two years, are on the same lofty level of literature—an achievement unique in the annals of Southwestern fiction.

Alan Le May is another western novelist who, like Will Levington Comfort, hacked away for years in the slick magazine jungles, until he achieved his finest work in *The Searchers* and *The Unforgiven,* novels of the Plains Indians—Comanches and Kiowas.

The only novel I know of about the Yaqui Indians of Sonora-Arizona, Kino's immemorial Pimería Alta, is *Hill of the Rooster* by Curry Holden, a heartbreaking story of the Mexicans' persecution of the Yaquis, which resulted finally in their flight across the border to settle in the village of Pascua, on the edge of Tucson. Like Oliver La Farge, Curry Holden turned from anthropology to fiction, in order better to express the truth as he saw and felt it.

These works of creative literature, as distinguished from the spate of journalistic pot-boiling "Westerns," are marked by their authors' possession of the gift of the three S's: the power to see, to sense, and to say.

There is of course a fourth S: sex, the absence or the presence of which in Southwestern literature has never been studied, at least to my knowledge. "Take all the pioneer women in the chronicles," Dobie once wrote to me, "not a single one of them has a breast, a flank, or a perfume in the mouth," whereas the women in later fictional works on the West are amply endowed and described. This change of interest and emphasis is a ripe theme for study.

## READING LIST

Frank G. Applegate. *Native Tales of New Mexico.* Philadelphia, Lippincott, 1932.

Elliott Arnold. *Blood Brother.* New York, Duell, Sloan and Pearce, 1947.

Mary Austin. *The American Rhythm.* New York, Harcourt, Brace, 1923.

Irwin R. Blacker. *Taos.* Cleveland, World, 1959.

Mary and Conrad Buff. *Hah-nee of the Cliff Dwellers.* Boston, Houghton Mifflin, 1956.

Willa Cather. *Death Comes for the Archbishop.* New York, Knopf, 1929.

Willa Cather. "Tom Outland's Story," in *The Professor's House.* New York, Knopf, 1925.

Will Levington Comfort. *Apache.* New York, Dutton, 1931.

Edwin Corle. *Fig Tree John.* New York, Liveright, 1935; Los Angeles, Ward Ritchie Press, 1955.

Edwin Corle. *People on the Earth.* New York, Random House, 1937.

Frank Hamilton Cushing. *Zuñi Breadstuff.* (Indian Notes and Monographs, v. 8) New York, Museum of the American Indian, Heye Foundation, 1920.

Erna Fergusson. *Dancing Gods; Indian Ceremonials of New Mexico and Arizona.* New York, Knopf, 1931. (Another edition, Albuquerque, University of New Mexico Press, 1957.)

Berard Haile. *Origin Legends of the Navaho Enemy Way.* Text and translation by Father Berard Haile. (Yale University Publications in Anthropology, v. 17) New Haven, Yale University Press, 1938.

Alice Corbin Henderson. *Brothers of Light, the Penitentes of the Southwest.* New York, Harcourt, Brace, 1937.

Zane Grey. *The Heritage of the Desert.* New York, Harper, 1910.

Zane Grey. *The Light of Western Stars.* New York, Harper, 1914.

Zane Grey. *The Rainbow Trail.* New York, Harper, 1915.

Zane Grey. *Riders of the Purple Sage.* New York, Harper, 1912.

Edgar Lee Hewett. *Ancient Life in the American Southwest.* Indianapolis, Bobbs-Merrill, 1930.

Frederick Webb Hodge. *Handbook of American Indians, North of Mexico.* 2 vols. (Bureau of American Ethnology, Bulletin no. 30) Washington, Government Printing Office, 1912.

Frederick Webb Hodge. *History of Hawikuh, New Mexico, one of the so-called Cities of Cíbola.* Los Angeles, The Southwest Museum, 1937.

Curry Holden. *Hill of the Rooster*. New York, Holt, 1956.

Alfred Vincent Kidder. *Introduction to the Study of Southwestern Archaeology, with a Preliminary Account of the Excavations at Pecos*. Rev. ed. New Haven, Yale University Press, 1962.

Alfred Vincent Kidder. *Pecos, New Mexico: Archaeological Notes*. (Papers of the Robert S. Peabody Foundation for Archaeology, v. 5) Andover, Mass., Phillips Academy, The Foundation, 1958.

Alfred Vincent Kidder. "Reminiscences in Southwestern Archaeology," in *Kiva*, v. 25, April 1960, pp. 1-32.

Oliver La Farge. *Laughing Boy*. Boston, Houghton Mifflin, 1929.

Alan Le May. *The Searchers*. New York, Harper, 1957.

Alan Le May. *The Unforgiven*. New York, Harper, 1957.

Frank McNitt. *The Indian Traders*. Norman, University of Oklahoma Press, 1962.

Frank McNitt. *Richard Wetherill: Anasazi*. Albuquerque, University of New Mexico Press, 1957.

Alice Marriott. *These are the People; Some Notes on the Southwestern Indians*. Santa Fe, Laboratory of Anthropology, 1949.

Washington Matthews. *Navaho Legends*. Collected and translated by Washington Matthews. (Memoirs of the American Folk-lore Society, v. 7) Boston, Houghton Mifflin, 1897.

*Navajo Yearbook*, No. 1, 1950/52—. Window Rock, Arizona, U.S. Bureau of Indian Affairs; Navajo Agency.

Gustav Erik Adolf Nordenskiöld. *The Cliff Dwellers of the Mesa Verde, Southwestern Colorado; Their Pottery and Implements*. Stockholm, P. A. Norstedt and Söner, 1893.

Edward H. Spicer. *Cycles of Conquest; the Impact of Spain, Mexico, and the U.S. on the Indians of the Southwest, 1533-1960*. Tucson, University of Arizona Press, 1962.

Don C. Talayesva. *Sun Chief, the Autobiography of a Hopi Indian*. New Haven, Yale University Press, 1942.

Ruth Murray Underhill. *Singing for Power, the Song Magic of the Papago Indians of Southern Arizona*. Berkeley, University of California Press, 1938.

Frank Waters. *The Man Who Killed the Deer*. Denver, University of Denver Press, 1942.

Frank Waters. *Masked Gods; Navaho and Pueblo Ceremonialism*. Albuquerque, University of New Mexico Press, 1950.

George Webb. *A Pima Remembers*. Tucson, University of Arizona Press, 1959.

## v. *The Way West*

LESS THAN a hundred fifty years ago the first trappers and traders made their way overland. Jedediah Smith is said to be the first to reach Southern California from Missouri. That was in 1826. He left a fragmentary journal without literary merit. The Comanches killed him in what is now Kansas. The only Southwestern trek to rank with Lewis and Clark's was the Anza expedition. The later Anglo influx to the west coast, culminating in the gold rush, was mostly by central routes.

All of the ways west have been intensively studied. There is an enormous literature about them in the great government reports and surveys of the nineteenth century. Carl I. Wheat, assisted by Dale L. Morgan, compiled the monumental set called *Mapping the Transmississippi West.* Henry R. Wagner's *The Plains and the Rockies* is the standard bibliography of the westward flow. A useful cartographic resume is J. Gregg Layne's *Western Wayfaring; Routes of Exploration and Trade in the American Southwest,* consisting of twenty-eight maps and historical texts on the principal routes, beginning with Pike's 1806 expedition and ending with the first transcontinental railroad in 1869. Edward S. Wallace's *The Great Reconaissance; Soldiers, Artists, and Scientists on the Frontier, 1848-1861,* is a good book on the boundary and railroad surveys and the wealth of documentation they produced.

Today one boards a jet in Chicago, loafs with nose to window, and in three hours sees it all pass below, a dream procession, a foreshortening of history. The land changes rapidly; the checkerboard of the Middle West jumbles, roughens, colors; the rivers go dry, the Rockies rear up; everything is tiny; and then the Angel City enfolds one in her drab robes.

How can we know what it was like to go it on foot, or horse, or wagon, taking months for what now takes hours? We can't. All we can do is to take a vantage point in the imagination or, if fortunate, on the land itself, in peace and silence, with a book or two, read and meditate and try to reverse the time stream, go back to the way it was when there were no roads, no friendly inhabitants, only hazards, often death.

I have such a vantage point to which I have been drawn many times in the past ten years. It is on the Santa Fe Trail, not far from its end in the City of the Holy Faith, on the highway and railroad which follows the old wagon trail along that last historic stretch, through the piñon forest, across the Pecos and lesser arroyos, from Las Vegas to Santa Fe. There at the double-track crossing of Ribera, near the midway point between Chicago and Los Angeles, I wait to see the east-west trains meet; and when they do, I experience an illumination in which all is clear and simple and made known. If I had not already declared Albuquerque to be the heart of my Southwest, I would say that it is here at Ribera on the Santa Fe, where the Pecos crosses, that one feels at the epicenter of Southwestern history.

He who would break out of the daily straightjacket must seek his own time and place of truth. Books help. Books are triggers to shoot us free, are bombs to blow us up and away. Inscription Rock, now known as El Morro National Monument, is such a place, an immemorial stopping point for Spaniards and Anglos bound for Arizona and California, its benison a water-hole in the Rock and grazing for hungry animals. On the lee side of El Morro, in the sandstone, travellers have carved inscriptions, begining with Juan de Oñate in 1605 and usually prefaced with the words *Pasó por aqui* (came this way). In the beginning, the inscriptions were often of calligraphic beauty; many have been effaced by wind and rain. During the nineteenth century the hasty whites, rushing for gold, scratched and scrawled names or initials without feeling for form or ceremony. In 1906 President Theodore Roosevelt, staunch defender of our natural heritage, declared El Morro a national monument; and ever since, it has been protected by a custodian.

Whatever may befall El Morro, and in time the elements will scour it clean, its inscriptions and descriptions are transfixed and preserved, as it were forever, in a book of great beauty, a labor of love by a Los Angeles electronics engineer, John M. Slater, who gathered all the known drawings and photographs and transcriptions and brought them together, at his own expense, in *El Morro,* printed by Saul and Lillian Marks of Los Angeles.

Go there with this book, and with Mary Austin's *Land of Journeys' Ending,* and read her chapter called "Paso por aqui," with its poignant peroration, "Here I shall haunt"; and then and there, if ever and anywhere, you will perceive history with clarity.

I know of no memorable novels of the Santa Fe and southern routes; no A. B. Guthrie has done for them what he did for the Oregon Trail in *The Big Sky* and *The Way West.* Harvey Fergusson's two novels, *Wolf Song* and *Grant of Kingdom,* are of the Sangre de Cristos around Taos; they are the classic novels of the southernmost mountain men.

The earliest narrative is an exciting blend of fact and fiction, the one written by James Ohio Pattie, who was trapping and trading in New Mexico and California in the 1820's, right after Jedediah Smith went that way. First published at Cincinnati in 1831, if sold now at auction in the original, Pattie's book would put your son (and daughter) through college.

Thirteen years later came Josiah Gregg's *Commerce of the Prairies, the* classic of the prairies and the Santa Fe Trail. Gregg knew more, saw clearer, wrote better than any others of his time and place; and so his work, oft reprinted, has assumed a commanding place in the literature of the Southwest.

In his foreword to the later *Diary and Letters,* Paul Horgan wrote, "Gregg was of the order of men who create literature out of their most daily preoccupations, that is, without a transfiguring act of the imagination;" and another New Mexican (now an Arizonan) Patricia Paylore wrote even more perceptively of Gregg, "No event which came within his view escaped his consideration and analysis. No aspect of strange custom or unusual habit failed to engage his interest. And everywhere he went, there also for our everlasting enrichment went his little bound notebooks. Even when he was dying of starvation in the wilderness of northern California, he enraged his companions by delaying their efforts to escape their plight with his computations of latitude and longitude, and the measurement of fallen redwood trees."

And as a clincher, in case you doubt the judgment of Horgan and Paylore, here is Dobie on Gregg: "He wrote not only the classic of the Santa Fe trade and trail, but one of the classics of bedrock Americana."

Of lesser scope but also a classic is Lewis H. Garrard's *Wah-to-yah and the Taos Trail.* First published in 1850 and oft reprinted, this narrative of a young man's adventures has the springtime freshness of youth. Garrard made the trip at seventeen and wrote his book soon thereafter; later he wrote nothing else of interest, making inevitable a comparison of him with R. H. Dana, Jr., and his *Two Years Before the Mast.* The latest reprint of *Wah-to-yah* has a foreword by A. B. Guthrie, which is almost gilding the lily.

Few are the early accounts of the Southwest by women observers. Susan Magoffin's is one of the best. Like Garrard, she was a youthful observer. Her diary of 1846-47 was written on her honeymoon; she was nineteen turned twenty. It was not published until 1926, seventy-one years after her death.

Susan Magoffin was in Santa Fe at the time her brother-in-law, Colonel James Magoffin, persuaded General Armijo to surrender the city bloodlessly to the Americans. Her diary is thus a prime source on "the year of decision," as De Voto called it. It is a shrewd and tender view of men and events.

One of the mystery men of the Southwest is H. M. T. Powell, known only by the journal he wrote of a Southwestern entrada. *The Santa Fe Trail to California, 1849-1852* was published the first and only time in 1931 by the Book Club of California in a noble folio, printed by the Grabhorn Press, and illustrated from Powell's own drawings of the trail. This book has become one of the most sought after works on the Southwest and should be reprinted. Powell came into Southern California via the Tucson and the Yuma crossing route. His entries are terse and laconic, his drawings simple and evocative.

Conner's *Joseph Reddeford Walker and the Arizona Adventure* is one of the fullest and most vivid accounts of the exploration of southern Arizona; and add to it the earlier J. Ross Browne's *Adventures in the Apache Country.*

I close this chapter with praise for an obscure modern book for which I have a high regard. *Crisscross Trails; Narrative of a Soil Surveyor* by Macy H. Lapham is a modest work, produced on the varitype, and yet it has those qualities of literature we seek: perception, absorptive capacity, stamina, felicitous expression. From 1899 until his retirement forty years later, Lapham crisscrossed the West and Southwest for the United States Department of Agriculture, pioneering of a later sort, surely, but imbued with the spirit of Gregg and the early ones who came to the scene with fresh and eager vision, permeated with feeling for history, both human and natural.

"As I sat at my window in the hotel," Lapham recalled of a mission that took him to Nogales, "the figure of a little Mexican woman carrying a load of lumber trotted by. This consisted of a half dozen thin boards neatly balanced on her head and extending some five or six feet to the front and rear. They swayed in unison with the movements of her body, creating a picture of rhythmic grace in the apparently effortless bearing of so heavy a burden."

## READING LIST

Mary Austin. *The Land of Journeys' Ending.* New York, Century, 1924.

Daniel E. Conner. *Joseph Reddeford Walker and the Arizona Adventure.* Norman, University of Oklahoma Press, 1956.

Lewis H. Garrard. *Wah-to-yah and the Taos Trail, or, Prairie Travel and Scalp Dances, with a look at los rancheros from Muleback and the Rocky Mountain Campfire.* Cincinnati, H. W. Derby and Co.; New York, A. S. Barnes and Co., 1850; Norman, University of Oklahoma Press, 1955.

Josiah Gregg. *Commerce of the Prairies: or, The Journal of a Santa Fe Trader, during eight expeditions across the great western prairies, and a residence of nearly nine years in northern Mexico.* 2 vols. New York, H. G. Langley, 1844; Norman, University of Oklahoma Press, 1954.

Josiah Gregg. *Diary and Letters.* 2 vols. Norman, University of Oklahoma Press, 1941-44.

A. B. Guthrie. *The Big Sky.* New York, William Sloane Associates, 1947.

A. B. Guthrie. *The Way West.* New York, William Sloane Associates, 1949.

Macy H. Lapham. *Crisscross Trails. Narrative of a Soil Surveyor.* Berkeley, Willis F. Berg, 1949.

J. Gregg Layne. *Western Wayfaring, Routes of Exploration and Trade in the American Southwest.* Los Angeles, Automobile Club of Southern California, 1954.

Susan Shelby Magoffin. *Down the Santa Fe Trail and Into Mexico; the Diary of Susan Shelby Magoffin, 1946-1847.* New Haven, Yale University Press, 1926; the same, 1962.

James Ohio Pattie. *The Personal Narrative of James O. Pattie, of Kentucky.* Cincinnati, E. H. Flint, 1831; Philadelphia, Lippincott, 1962.

Patricia Paylore. "Inside Oklahoma," in *The Southwest of the Bookman,* pp. 34-39. (Occasional Paper no. 11) Los Angeles, University of California Library, 1959.

H. M. T. Powell. *The Santa Fe Trail to California, 1849-1852.* San Francisco, The Book Club of California, 1931.

John M. Slater. *El Morro, Inscription Rock, New Mexico. The Rock Itself, the Inscriptions Thereon, and the Travelers who Made Them.* Preface by Lawrence Clark Powell. Los Angeles, The Plantin Press, 1961.

Henry R. Wagner. *The Plains and the Rockies; a Bibliography of Original Narratives of Travel and Adventure, 1800-1865,* revised and extended by Charles L. Camp. San Francisco, The Grabhorn Press, 1937.

Edward S. Wallace. *The Great Reconnaissance; Soldiers, Artists, and Scientists on the Frontier, 1848-1861.* Boston, Little, Brown, 1955.

Carl I. Wheat. *Mapping the Transmississippi West, 1540-1861.* 5 vols. San Francisco, Institute of Historical Cartography, 1957-1963.

## vi. *Personal Landscapes*

BY "personal landscape" I mean an individualistic, instinctive response to a region which results in a book of essays or description or reminiscence, or novel or stories; in any case, an affirmation of love and faith—the opposite of the hack job, the "quickie," commissioned by magazine or publisher, or the academic exercise done to satisfy a degree-requirement. I mean the vital and the organic as opposed to the mechanistic or the artificial.

It does not require being a native son or long resident to write truly about a place. What is required is a writer's ability to root, to send down (and up) his sources of nourishment and strength. See how swiftly this was done by two professional writers, long practiced in their art, who came to the Southwest and soon wrote about the region with perception, fidelity, and power—D. H. Lawrence in New Mexico, Joseph Wood Krutch in Arizona. It is the equipment a writer brings to a landscape which determines what he can mine from it. There are two kinds of root systems that nourish a writer: the deep tap root of the redwood, the lateral surface system of the mesquite. An example of the former is Harvey Fergusson; of the latter, D. H. Lawrence. Both can produce literature.

The first of my "personal landscape" artists is Charles F. Lummis, that egocentric, idealistic dam' yankee who trudged from Ohio to Southern California and parlayed the experience into a shelf of books before he died in 1927. Lummis returned repeatedly to New Mexico, conducting a lifelong love affair with the land of the pueblos. He once lived at Isleta, the river pueblo below Albuquerque. He was the first to write personally with enthusiasm about the Southwest. He was the first to use the phrases "The Southwest" and "See America First." His *Mesa, Canyon, and Pueblo* could have been placed as well in my first chapter, with Erna Fergusson's *Our Southwest,* for it is the first comprehensive book on the region. And it is *personal* throughout; one is never unaware of Lummis's tendency to self glorification, even when he is ostensibly being the most objective; whereas Miss Fergusson never intrudes herself between region and reader, is discreet, fastidious.

The colorful Lummis has never been done biographical justice. A UCLA dissertation by Edwin Bingham, subtitled *Editor of the Southwest,* concentrates on Lummis's magazine *Land of Sunshine,* and because it was written under the direction of John Walton Caughey, it is well written and readable. Professor Dudley Gordon has been shadow-boxing with the Lummis papers in the Southwest Museum, warming up to write a "life and letters," but thus far he has not landed any solid punches.

Lummis was not given to mysticism. His writing is factual. He went to sources. He was the first to make recordings of Indian and Spanish folk songs and chants. D. H. Lawrence *was* a mystic. Indians and landscape moved him to brood on the cosmos and to write *The Plumed Serpent,* a religious-philosophical-political novel about Mexico. In *Mornings in Mexico,* a book of essays, the novel *St. Mawr* and the stories *The Princess* and *The Woman Who Rode Away,* are found Lawrence's personal landscapes of New Mexico and Arizona.

His landscape is centered around Taos, the focal point of northern New Mexico, immemorial trappers' rendezvous of the southernmost Rockies, magnetic pole to which are ever drawn artists of brush and pen. From the viewpoint of his Kiowa Ranch, northwest of Taos, on the aspened slope of Lobo Mountain, Lawrence enjoyed one of the most fabulous of New Mexico's panoramas; and after he had returned to Europe in 1928, he wrote nostalgically of this view he was never to see again:

"There are all kinds of beauty in the world, thank God, though ugliness is homogeneous. How lovely is Sicily, with Calabria across the sea like an opal, and Etna with her snow in a world above and beyond! How lovely is Tuscany, with little red tulips wild among the corn; or bluebells at dusk in England, or mimosa in clouds of pure yellow among the grey-green dun foliage of Australia, under a soft, blue unbreathed sky!

"But for *greatness* of beauty I have never experienced anything like New Mexico. All those mornings when I went with a hoe along the ditch to the cañon, at the ranch, and stood, in the fierce, proud silence of the Rockies, on their foothills, to look far over the desert to the blue mountains of Arizona, blue as chalcedony, with the sage-brush desert sweeping grey-blue in between, dotted with tiny cube-crystals of houses, the vast amphitheatre of lofty indomitable desert, sweeping around to the ponderous Sangre de Cristo mountains on the east, and coming up flush at the pine-dotted foot-hills of the Rockies!"

Another lyrical description of the Taos plain occurs in *Grant of Kingdom,* when Fergusson's protagonist comes back to it in the spring:

"It was a triangular splotch of bright cultivated green, spread like a shining robe across the dull gray and purple of sage and lava. Three bright clear streams, coming down from the mountains to meet and plunge into the Rio Grande, gave it the water of life, and it shimmered and quivered and sang with life in the May sunshine."

North and east of Taos lie the lands of the Maxwell Grant. There are sober histories of it, none of which, however, contains the essential truth of a mere novel, *Grant of Kingdom,* a book I believe will be read to the end of New Mexican time, when the mere histories are gathering dust, if not dust themselves. Most of Harvey Fergusson's books are out of print; needed is a collected edition of his works, novels and other.

Mabel Dodge Luhan is another writer long identified with Taos. It was she who lured Lawrence to New Mexico and gave him Kiowa Ranch in return for the manuscript of *Sons and Lovers*. This ranch is the last resting place of Lawrence and Frieda, his beloved wife who outlived him twenty-six years; it now belongs to the University of New Mexico and is maintained as a writers' retreat. Most of Mrs. Luhan's energies went into her role as artistic arbiter of Taos; but she did write an evocation of her adopted homeland in *Winter in Taos,* as well as a good book about the artists there.

Down river the Santa Fe landscape has produced its share of "bookscapes." In 1943-44 the *Colorado Magazine* published in serial form reminiscences I find to be one of the most feeling and knowing of all these personal testaments. They consist of the memoirs of Marian Sloan Russell, as dictated by her in her old age (her life span was 1845-1937) to her daughter-in-law, and collected later in book form. This lady miraculously found the language of literature, as in this passage wherein she recalled the first time she was alone with the man she loved.

It was in the year 1864, "When September rolled around, Mother moved again to Santa Fe. I was sick at heart because so far she had never permitted Richard and me a moment alone together. Always we were chaperoned; always mother or some elderly couple was with us. Only our eyes could speak of the dawning love in our young hearts.

"We moved to Santa Fe and a whole week passed, and I had not heard from my lover. Then one morning a great caravan was sighted coming in from Fort Union. I thought surely there would be a letter for me from Richard, so I dressed up a bit and walked to the post office. I stood waiting among the jostling throng until my turn came at the window. There was no letter for Miss Marian Sloan. No news from my tall lieutenant.

"I recall that I had dressed with special care that morning. My dress was of factory-woven cloth, in what they then called cotton challis. It was a glorious dress of a soft golden color. It had a tight little bodice buttoned down the front with jewelled buttons. The sleeves were long and close-fitting. At my throat was cream lace ruching and mother's cameo brooch. The skirt of my long dress had many fluttering ruffles. That day at the post office lies in my memory as faint and sweet as the scent of old lavender. I had turned sadly from the post office window and was starting homeward when someone came up behind me and drew my hand through his arm. I turned quickly. It was Richard. He had come with the emigrant train from Fort Union. My heart overflowing with joy, I went where he led me and soon we were standing beneath the great wooden arch on the outskirts of Santa Fe. We were alone for the first time since the day of our meeting.

"Eastward the wide trail flowed like a river. From the blue hills came the tinkle of sheep bells. It was the close of an Indian summer day; it was also the close of my girlhood."

After she left California, following the rape of the Owens River Valley by Los Angeles and her prophecy of ultimate doom of the city, Mary Austin lived the rest of her life in Santa Fe. From this long residence—she died in 1934—came a stream of books, in none of which did she reach the peak of her two California "personal landscapes," *The Land of Little Rain* and *The Flock,* although her *Land of Journeys' Ending,* consisting of essays about New Mexico and Arizona, comes the closest.

In T. M. Pearce's biography, *The Beloved House* and in her own autobiography *Earth Horizon,* may be found material for a study of Mary Austin's creative arc. She was the victim of the most deadly of Cyril Connolly's "enemies of promise": success, with its attendant evils, self-consciousness of being a literary figure, public admiration, etc.

Worth study is Santa Fe as a literary center. Witter Bynner has lived there for nearly half a century, yet has not been moved to write of the region more than a slim volume of poems called *Indian Earth.* Haniel Long founded the regional publishing house which flourished for a time; but other than *Piñon Country,* he never created a "personal landscape"; and the book he was working on when he died, was a novel about his roots in the East.

Another Harvard man, Oliver La Farge, is a long-time resident of Santa Fe, and his career subsequent to his best selling *Laughing Boy* of 1929 offers another arc for study. Stories, novels, a slight autobiography, and many good works on behalf of the Indians, may well be outweighed by one book of essays, *Behind the Mountains,* about his Spanish-American wife's family home at Rociada, in the Sangre de Cristos northeast of Santa Fe.

That same area, somewhat more to the east, is the setting of Frank Waters' novel *People of the Valley,* one of the least appreciated and, in my opinion, one of the best of all books (novel or otherwise) about landscape and love in New Mexico. Waters' work has an earthy virility absent from the Luhan-Austin-Bynner-Long-La Farge "literary" works.

Peggy Pond Church is a native New Mexican writer "discovered" by Haniel Long, who issued volumes of her poetry over the Writers' Editions imprint; and her *Familiar Journey* poetically evokes the region's seasonal changes. A larger theme gripped her, however, in a book of prose, *The House at Otowi Bridge,* the life and letters of Edith Warner, a Pennsylvania spinster who settled at a bridge point on the Rio Grande, three miles from San Ildefonso Pueblo below Los Alamos, with an Indian man as companion; and then when Los Alamos was transformed into an atomic bomb laboratory, made a tea-house for the scientists "on the hill." Edith Warner's story, based on her letters and diary, is poignantly told by Peggy Church, a writer supremely fitted to tell it, for her father founded and her husband was headmaster of Los Alamos School, the institution known to Dr. Robert Oppenheimer, which led to the massive take-over of the Pajarito Plateau by the bomb-makers, and she lived there for twenty years.

*The House at Otowi Bridge* is a beautiful book in conception and content, and in format by Roland Dickey, New Mexico's finest book designer.

Down river from Albuquerque the land has not been evoked in the same way as the Upper Sonoran zone of the north. Agnes Morley Cleaveland's *No Life for a Lady* is the best personal land-scape of the cattle country around Datil. The stories of Eugene Man-love Rhodes, set in the Rio Grande country around Socorro, are true to the land and life of this region. No one has yet written memorably of Cloudcroft, of Alamogordo, or of Roswell—landscapes awaiting their ultimate evocation. Perhaps Conrad Richter's novel, *The Sea of Grass,* is the truest book about the plains where New Mexico and Texas meet.

C. L. Sonnichsen, Dean of Texas Western College, is also the dean of historical writers about this region of southeastern New Mexico. His anthology, *The Southwest in Life and Literature,* is a masterful book of extracts from forty-three writers.

My favorite book about this area and the one that comes the closest to meeting my definition of "personal landscape", is *Captive Mountain Waters* by Dorothy Jensen Neal, an account of bringing water by pipeline to the arid lands below.

Ross Calvin's *Sky Determines* is a classic book, central in New Mexican literature. It sees the state as a whole, is sensitive to the changes of landscape and weather from the plains of Roswell and Clovis (Dr. Calvin was an Episcopal minister in the latter town) to the mountainous Southwest, the river valley, the high north, and the colored west, the Navajo country where New Mexico blends into Arizona. Here is another Harvard-man come west for his health who came closer to the psyche of his adopted state than most of those who were born and lived their lives in New Mexico. We must cross into Arizona to the books of Joseph Wood Krutch to find another writer who has written as well of natural environment in the Southwest.

Krutch, also a university man from the "far East," takes the same wide view of Arizona that Calvin does of New Mexico. Krutch's books range from *Grand Canyon* in the north to *The Desert Year* and *The Voice of the Desert* in the south around Tucson where he makes his home; and even farther south and west to Baja California, of which his *Forgotten Peninsula* is one of the best evocations. Both Ross Calvin and Joseph Krutch are of the "cool school" of Erna Fergusson. Their landscapes are personal to the extent that their intellectual and moral beliefs about life in the Southwest are inseparable from their descriptive prose. They are impersonally personal—a paradox I hope will not be incomprehensible.

Frank Dobie's later books, notably *The Longhorns* and *The Mustangs,* have more of him in them than the earlier *Coronado's Children* and *Apache Gold and Yaqui Silver,* his accounts of lost mines and buried treasure. Less well known, and his own favorite among his books, is *Tongues of the Monte,* a personal landscape of his travels across the border into Chihuahua.

Another border book, which bears the strong personality of its creator, is Tom Lea's novel *The Wonderful Country,* a love poem in prose to the Texas–Mexico border country, the cowboys and soldiers, and to Lágrimas, the noblest Southwestern horse of them all.

Thus far I have stressed the similarities that make New Mexico and Arizona the heart of the Southwest: their Spanish origins, common Indian tribes, configurations and climate, far distances and few people, and a literature that links their cultures.

Books should be written also on their differences, on the effects of such two dissimiliar river systems as the Grande and the Colorado; on the way the two Spanish pueblos, Santa Fe and Tucson, grew, the one preserving its Spanish character, the other becoming anglicized; on the economies of Albuquerque and Phoenix; on the effect of Texas on New Mexico, particularly in the southeast, and of Southern California on Arizona, notably the power struggle for the Colorado River and the influx of Los Angeles capital into the Salt River Valley. Books are called for also about absentee capital development of Arizona's mines, railroads, agriculture, animal husbandry, banks, and mercantile houses. Jews and Mormons have been major architects of Arizona's economy, and still are; their contributions have yet to be thoroughly assessed. It is time, I say, for writers to stop playing Cowboy and Indian.

Arizona has no Taos, no Santa Fe. Scottsdale is a synthetic artists colony; Old Tucson a phony replica of the stereotype Old West. Apart from the University, Tucson has small culture, no gallery of Southwestern art, no outdoor opera; and save for Dr. Krutch, no spokesman against the "progress" which is turning the desert into a tract-house blight.

"The climate of this region," wrote Frank Lloyd Wright, "abhors the 'box' "; and yet that is what is being built by the tens of thousands, and not only in Arizona but round about Albuquerque and El Paso. Smog which has hitherto been regarded as the curse only of Los Angeles (is *it* the fulfillment of Mary Austin's prophecy of doom?) is now dirtying the sky over Phoenix, Tucson, Albuquerque, and El Paso.

Arizona has never bred a family like the Fergussons, has never attracted and retained literary figures such as Luhan, Long, Austin, Bynner, Calvin, Horgan, Foster, Waters. Tucson's finest novelist, Richard Summers, whose book *Dark Madonna* is a powerful work on the Spanish minority, is disregarded in his home town. De Grazia, Tucson's most original artist, is unhonored there.

Southern Arizona's most versatile writer over the years is Ross Santee, but the region has not held him. He has long since lived in

Delaware. Santee's *Cowboy* and *Apache Land,* his *Hardrock and Silver Sage* and *The Bubbling Spring* are regional evocations of power and beauty, illustrated by himself with black and white drawings of great economy. His work may be seen in many issues of *Arizona Highways.*

Carl Lumholtz's *New Trails in Mexico* should not mislead one by its title to expect a work only on Mexico. It is about the border country of Sonora–Arizona, the Papaguería, the "waste land" of the Papago Indians and their sacred peak Baboquívari. Likewise Godfrey Sykes' *A Westerly Trend,* one of the few works of literature published in Tucson, is a wanderer's book about southwestern Arizona that evokes a superficially barren landscape actually of complex beauty.

The best of all Arizona personal landscapes is Martha Summerhayes' *Vanished Arizona,* the reminiscenses of a young army wife of the 1870's and 1880's. First published in 1908 and reprinted several times, as recently as 1962, this is the classic account of the Apache frontier seen with a woman's clear, brave, and loving gaze, a book to shelve next to Susan Magoffin's evocation of the New Mexican frontier.

I have followed Martha Summerhayes' trail, with her book on the seat beside me, from Yuma to Fort Apache, from Ehrenburg to Tucson, Fort Whipple, and Camp Verde, seeing what she saw with her eyes and with mine, with the double vision given to a reading traveller, a travelling reader; and in an essay called "Winter Days with Martha Summerhayes", I reported that much of her Arizona has not vanished, in spite of the nostalgic peroration with which she ends *Vanished Arizona:*

"Sometimes I hear the still voices of the desert: they seem to be calling me through the echoes of the past. I hear, in fancy, the wheels of the ambulance crunching the small broken stones of the *malpais,* or grating swiftly over the gravel of the smooth white roads of the riverbottoms. I hear the rattle of the ivory rings on the harness of the six-mule team; I see the soldiers marching on ahead. I see my white tent, so inviting after a long day's journey.

"But how vain these fancies! Railroad and automobile have annihilated distance, the army life of those years is past and gone, and Arizona, as we knew it, has vanished from the face of the earth."

Choose your own book of history or reminiscences of the Southwest and let it be your guidebook to past and present. A friend of mine did this with the English adventurer Frederick Ruxton's book called *Life in the Far West;* and with the book on the seat beside him ascended the Rio Grande from El Paso to Taos; and thence by another route he followed Ruxton high into the Rockies of Colorado.

In "Sky, Sun and Water" I went over the early trails of Hodge in the Southwest; and I had the supreme privilege of reporting on my journey to the old man himself at a dinner meeting in honor of his 89th birthday. My "Revista Nueva Mexicana" is another travel report one can verify for himself, if he will leave library for landscape.

*Landscape* magazine's *Autoguide to Northern New Mexico* is an example of a happy marriage of past and present, far more meaningful than the ordinary Chamber of Commerce booster booklet. In the early years of the Santa Fe Railroad, Fred Harvey published a series of good guide booklets on the Southwest.

## READING LIST

Mary Austin. *Earth Horizon, Autobiography.* Boston, Houghton Mifflin, 1932.

Edwin R. Bingham. *Charles F. Lummis, Editor of the Southwest.* San Marino, Huntington Library, 1955.

Witter Bynner. *Indian Earth.* New York, Knopf, 1929.

Ross Calvin. *Sky Determines; an Interpretation of the Southwest.* New York, Macmillan, 1934; Albuquerque, University of New Mexico Press, 1948.

Peggy Pond Church. *Familiar Journey.* Santa Fe, Writers' Editions, 1936.

Peggy Pond Church. *The House at Otowi Bridge. The Story of Edith Warner and Los Alamos.* Albuquerque, University of New Mexico Press, 1959.

Agnes Morley Cleaveland. *No Life for a Lady.* Boston, Houghton Mifflin, 1941.

J. Frank Dobie. *Apache Gold and Yaqui Silver.* Boston, Little, Brown, 1939.

J. Frank Dobie. *Coronado's Children; Tales of Lost Mines and Buried Treasures of the Southwest.* Dallas, The Southwest Press, 1930.

J. Frank Dobie. *The Longhorns.* Boston, Little, Brown, 1941.

J. Frank Dobie. *The Mustangs.* Boston, Little, Brown, 1952.

J. Frank Dobie. *Tongues of the Monte.* Garden City, New York Doubleday, Doran, 1935.

Joseph Wood Krutch. *The Desert Year.* New York, William Sloane Associates, 1952.

Joseph Wood Krutch. *The Forgotten Peninsula; a Naturalist in Baja California.* New York, William Sloane Associates, 1961.

Joseph Wood Krutch. *Grand Canyon; Today and all its Yesterdays.* New York, William Sloane Associates, 1958.

Joseph Wood Krutch. *The Voice of the Desert, a Naturalist's Interpretation.* New York, William Sloane Associates, 1955.

Oliver La Farge. *Behind the Mountains.* Boston, Houghton Mifflin, 1956.

*Landscape Autoguide to Northern New Mexico.* Tour I: Santa Fe to Taos. Santa Fe, *Landscape Magazine,* 1962.

D. H. Lawrence. *Mornings in Mexico.* New York, Knopf, 1927.

D. H. Lawrence. "New Mexico," in *Phoenix; the Posthumous Papers of D. H. Lawrence.* New York, Viking, 1936.

D. H. Lawrence. *St. Mawr, together with the Princess.* London, Secker, 1925.

D. H. Lawrence. *The Woman Who Rode Away, and Other Stories.* New York, Knopf, 1928.

Tom Lea. *The Wonderful Country.* Boston, Little Brown, 1952.

Mabel Dodge Luhan. *Winter in Taos.* New York, Harcourt, Brace, 1935.

Carl Lumholtz. *New Trails in Mexico; An Account of One Year's Exploration in North-western Sonora, Mexico, and South-western Arizona, 1909-1910.* New York, Scribner, 1912.

Charles F. Lummis. *Mesa, Cañon, and Pueblo; our wonderland of the Southwest, its Marvels of Nature, its Pageant of the Earth Building, its Strange People, its Centuried Romance.* New York, Century, 1925.

Dorothy Jensen Neal. *Captive Mountain Waters.* El Paso, Texas Western Press, 1961.

T. M. Pearce. *The Beloved House.* Caldwell, Idaho, Caxton, 1940.

Lawrence Clark Powell. "Revista Nueva Mexicana," in *Books in My Baggage, Adventures in Reading and Collecting.* Cleveland, World, 1960.

Lawrence Clark Powell. "Sky, Sun, and Water," in *Books West Southwest. Essays on Writers, Their Books, and Their Land.* Los Angeles, The Ward Ritchie Press, 1957.

Lawrence Clark Powell. "Winter Days with Martha Summerhayes," in *Arizona Highways,* Nov. 1961, pp. 2-7.

Eugene Manlove Rhodes. *Best Novels and Stories.* With an Introduction by J. Frank Dobie. Boston, Houghton Mifflin, 1949.

Marian Sloan Russell. "Memoirs of Marian Russell," in *Colorado Magazine,* May, July, Sept., Nov. 1943, pp. 81-95, 140-154, 181-196, 226-238; Jan., March, May 1944, pp. 29-37, 62-74, 101-112; also *Land of Enchantment,* Evanston, Branding Iron Press, 1954.

George F. Ruxton. *Life in the Far West.* Norman, University of Oklahoma Press, 1951.

George F. Ruxton. *Adventures in Mexico and the Rocky Mountains.* New York, Harper, 1848.

Ross Santee. *Apache Land.* New York, Scribner, 1947.

Ross Santee. *The Bubbling Spring.* New York, Scribner, 1949.

Ross Santee. *Cowboy.* New York, Cosmopolitan Book Corp., 1928.

Ross Santee. *Hardrock and Silver Sage.* New York, Scribner, 1951.

C. L. Sonnichsen. *The Southwest in Life and Literature.* New York, Devin-Adair, 1962.

Martha Summerhayes. *Vanished Arizona; Recollections of my Army Life.* Philadelphia, Lippincott, 1908; Salem, Mass., Salem Press Co., 1911; Tucson, Arizona Silhouettes, 1960.

Richard Summers. *Dark Madonna.* Caldwell, Idaho, Caxton, 1937.

Godfrey Sykes. *A Westerly Trend, Being a Veracious Chronicle of More than Sixty Years of Joyous Wandering, Mainly in Search of Space and Sunshine.* Tucson, Arizona Pioneers' Historical Society, 1944.

Frank Waters. *People of the Valley.* Denver, Alan Swallow, *c*1941; the same, 1962.

## vii. *The Southwest of the Artists*

THERE have been artists in the Southwest as long as there have been men. Motives change; the creative impulse begins in religion and is ceremonial or functional; and ends as a leisure or play occupation, as decoration. From pictographs on canyon walls art proceeds to cocktail lounge and airport murals. Banks and insurance companies in the Southwest today feature frescoes in which the history of the region is pictured as culminating in them. An artists' colony starts as an isolated community of genuines (Taos) and ends in a center for the smart set, turning out slick copies for tourists (Palm Springs-Scottsdale).

A similar change can be observed in the native arts since the Anglos came. Navajos and Apaches, the Pueblos of the river and mesa, the desert tribes, all have known artists among them, creative men and women who were not satisfied merely to weave plain rugs or to plait simple baskets. Form, design, color were wedded with function; and today in museums throughout the Southwest can be seen Navajo blankets of a century ago as mellow to the eye as any Persian rug; or pristine pueblo pottery; Hopi wedding baskets of rainbow-hues; Apache storage baskets tall as a man; Pima, Papago, Yuman, and Mojave reed work shaped to beauty unsurpassed by any Grecian urn.

The silver and turquoise jewelry of Navajo and Zuñi is so

widely copied that only an expert can tell if what he is seeing, outside a museum, was made in Zuñi or Prague.

It is late to begin to collect the blankets and basketry and jewelry of yesterday's Indian craftsmen, but it is not too late to see collections of it or to read books about it. There are museums in the Southwest, never crowded, quiet oases of beauty, where one may see these creations of high native art. In Santa Fe, the Museum of Folk Art features historic collections of rugs, baskets, pottery, jewelry, as well as annual shows of contemporary folk art by the Spanish, Indian, and Anglo peoples of New Mexico. In Flagstaff the Museum of Northern Arizona, in Phoenix the Heard Museum, and in Tucson the Arizona State Museum, display classics of aboriginal art. The Southwest Museum in Los Angeles has rich collections begun by its founder, Charles F. Lummis; and in Albuquerque the Harvey Museum at the Alvarado is packed with treasures.

There is no single comprehensive book on the Indian arts of the Southwest. Frederick Dockstader's *Indian Art in America* is devoted to the entire country and is a sumptuous, expensive volume. There is no lack of books on the individual arts, and I shall single out a few of the best. John Adair's *The Navajo and Pueblo Silversmiths* is the fruit of the author's manifold interest in the history, anthropology, and aesthetics of this craft, and it is illustrated from photographs of jewelry and its makers. Arthur Woodward's *Navajo Silversmithing* is written also by one who knows from long study and observation.

Before his untimely death in 1941 at the age of 42, Charles Amsden of the Southwest Museum wrote a scholarly, beautiful, and lasting work on textiles: *Navajo Weaving, its Technic and History,* with a foreword by Frederick Webb Hodge, is *the* book on the subject.

Bert Robinson's *The Basket Weavers of Arizona* is a valuable monograph on the work of that state's eight basket-making tribes. The literature of Indian pottery is extensive. Alice Marriott's *Maria, the Potter of San Ildefonso* is about a creative woman of strong character who has become famous as a ceramicist. There is irony in the location of her pueblo, at the foot of Los Alamos; down below, one woman making pots; up above, many men making bombs. Who will prevail?

Between the Indians and the Anglos are the Spanish-Americans of New Mexico, who have produced art forms of their own, beautifully combining the functional and the decorative. Roland Dickey's *New Mexico Village Arts* is a beautiful book on all kinds of folk work. E. Boyd's *Saints and Saint Makers* is the best monograph on *santos* and *santeros;* and her catalogue, *Popular Arts of Colonial New Mexico,* to illustrate the collections in the Museum of New Mexico, is one to shelve alongside Dickey. Paul Horgan's *The Saint Maker's Christmas Eve,* is a charming story. Patricinio Barela of Taos is a contemporary *santero* of primitive genius. Mildred and Judson Crews, writers and publishers of Taos, have described his work in a monograph.

In the nineteenth century, English and American artists came west with private and government expeditions and created a wealth of frontier art, depicting Indians, buffaloes, cattle, horses, soldiers, and plain landscape. Remington and Russell are the most famous of these Western artists, and there are books aplenty on both. The best roundup of frontier art is *Artists and Illustrators of the Old West* by Robert A. Taft of the University of Kansas.

This brings us to the turn of the century and the rise of the art colony. Taos was the first, I suppose because of its isolation and setting and freedom from artistic and social pretensions. Worth study is the phenomenon of the southwestern art colony, where and how they started, who made them, who took them over. A good start was made by Van Deren Coke in *Taos and Santa Fe,* a beautiful catalog of paintings by New Mexican artists, 1882-1942.

Mabel Luhan's *Taos and its Artists* is an account of that colony which a later influx of imitators and copiers and just plain phonies has not entirely ruined. Its neighbor, Santa Fe to the south, has been more urbanized, organized, socialized, but Taos is still far enough from main roads and airports to offer the maximum seclusion and minimum sociability the ambivalent artist requires.

Eric Sloane was a member of the Taos colony in the 1920's, then went east to a career as an illustrator. In the 1950's he came back to see what time had wrought on the rendezvous beloved of mountain men; and in his book *Return to Taos,* he wrote a moving account of return and change.

Today there are little galleries in Taos and Santa Fe where one may look at contemporary paintings and sculpture. I find such looking alluring in the same way I am drawn to second-hand bookshops, seeking the pearl-in-oyster, the gold-in-gravel; and although I have no deep response to an abstract Southwest, neither do I care for literal depictions of nature, preferring instead plain photography.

How is a painter to depict the Southwest, its variety of configuration and color? Should he seek the eternal verities by use of a few etched lines, a few primary hues? Nothing depresses me more than a gallery hung with gaudy efforts to copy desert sands and skies. There are books on how to paint the Southwest. There is a water-color painting school in Tucson. There are clubs whose members go into the desert, set up stool and easel, paint and palette, and copy what they see. I am not against this; it is good therapy for those who do it; but let us not mistake this activity for creative and lasting art.

*Who* sees is more important than *what's* seen. The filters of personal character through which the artist passes images of the visual world into the chambers of his creative being may, rarely, give originality to his work, but only rarely. Character determines. Originality is the supreme quality in all the arts. If it is present, the battle is not over; then the problem is of growth—of how to transcend success and break new ground. Few do it.

Peter Hurd of San Patricio and Tom Lea of El Paso are the best known painters of the southern Rio Grande country. They have done public works in New Mexico and Texas and much book illustration. (Incidentally, there is need for a guide book to public works of art in the Southwest—murals, fountains, monuments, galleries, etc.) Their Southwest is more literal than abstract and yet by simplification and re-arrangement, it is removed from the school of mere copying. Dobie has written the best account of Tom Lea as an artist in an introduction to a portfolio of reproductions of Lea's paintings. Paul Horgan's evaluation of Peter Hurd has been reprinted as the foreword to the Roswell Museum's catalog of Hurd's work, of which it has a permanent collection.

The Southwest has yet to produce an Andrew Wyeth.

In Arizona Ted de Grazia of Tucson is the most original of that state's moderns. Morenci-born, an educated primitive who has gone to the Yaquis, the Pimas, and the Papagos for brotherhood and inspiration, De Grazia's poignant Indians and Anglos, his silk screen booklets called *Arizona South,* and his drawings of Father Kino, all form an original conception of his arid environment. De Grazia's most original creation however, is the adobe chapel to Nuestra Señora de Guadelupe, built by himself with help from Indian friends, in the Catalina foothills near Tucson. Unrecognized by the Roman Catholic Church, into which De Grazia was born, menaced by subdivision and highway, this chapel is a testament of this artist's faith, a perfect place to hold Quaker meetings, with no preacher to disturb one's meditation.

Raymond Carlson, the editorial genius of *Arizona Highways,* has collected the work of his favorite moderns in *Gallery of Western Paintings,* and included representations of the painter I find most characteristic of the Southwest I know and love. He is Maynard Dixon, born at Fresno, California, in 1875, died at Tucson in 1946. Dixon was an original, who kept growing, kept moving along. Although for public buildings in California he painted historical murals —see the State Library in Sacramento, the Post Office in Canoga Park —his Arizona landscapes and characters came from a deeper source. In 1907 Dixon painted four panels for the Southern Pacific Station in Tucson, although in the course of station remodelling, they disappeared some twenty years ago. In *Maynard Dixon, Painter of the West,* Arthur Millier, the former art critic of the *Los Angeles Times,* includes a brief biography, a list of Dixon's exhibitions and locations of his murals and privately owned paintings, and reproductions of his work. Dixon's style, according to Millier, is "that quality which, in a life or a work of art, is the sign of confident and well balanced mastery of thought, feeling, and technical procedure. . . . The long lines, undisguised rhythms and clear color-tones of a Dixon painting announce that it is unmistakably his work. His signature on a painting seems almost superfluous. Maynard Dixon's true signature on a canvas is the style which pervades it."

Another account of Maynard Dixon's long growth was written by Don Louis Perceval, the London-born artist, who used Dixon's early sketches and drawings to illustrate a long article contributed to *The Brand Book, No. 8.* published by the Los Angeles Corral of the Westerners. From it we learn of Dixon's solitary visits at the turn of the century to the Navajo country, and we discover the sources of feeling and observation which led to the simplifications of his mature work.

Don Perceval also knew the north country from early years and in his *Navajo Sketch Book,* with text by Clay Lockett, we have the most beautiful book ever printed in Arizona—but more of this in the next chapter.

Another painter also in some ways a disciple of Maynard Dixon, is the Swiss-born Conrad Buff who, with his wife Mary as author, has produced several lithographic children's books of the Southwest; to the one on the Mesa Verde we have already referred. Their *Elf Owl* is about a desert spring in the Papaguería, flanked by a saguaro in which the little owl has his nest.

We own two oils by Conrad Buff I would not trade for all the Remingtons and Russells ever painted. One is of Maynard Dixon's cool-house, a buff-colored rock building with a turquoise door, placed in a rocky hillside at Mt. Carmel in southern Utah, under cottonwoods and blue sky—the purest Southwest in color and configuration.

The other Buff is of the confluence of the Green and the Colorado rivers, at the junction of the two streams, one out of Colorado, the other out of Utah, which give the mainstream the power to make its deep way to the Gulf. Nor literal nor abstract, it partakes of both styles, its primary colors blue of sky; red, white and purple of cliffs and mesas; green of water.

I have a Dixon too, but it is not strictly Southwestern. "Approaching Storm, California Coast Range" shows a green-brown valley floor and blue mountains, under a broken blue-gray sky. It might be the Salinas Valley, looking west to the Santa Lucias. It too I cherish above all the cowboy, Indian, and military paintings of earlier artists.

It remains to consider a few Southwestern photographers whose use of the camera is creative in that when we look at their pictures, we see what we did not perceive before with our own eyes.

One of the earliest was Adam Clark Vroman, the Pasadena Kodak dealer and bookseller, whose shop was to grow eventually into the largest in the Southwest. I was Vroman's shipping clerk after graduation from college; and years later, the firm asked me to write a brief history to mark the opening of a new store. I had never known anything of A. C. Vroman, who died in 1916; and it was not until I went to the Pasadena Public Library to see how they had used a $10,000 bequest from Vroman for the purchase of art books, that I discovered a mounted set of photographs he had made of southwestern scenes—of the pueblos and their ceremonies, of landscapes, of the Enchanted Mesa and Hodge's famous ascent of it. They were of stunning beauty.

I called on Dr. Hodge to ask if he knew what had happened to the Vroman negatives and learned from him that they had been sold by Vroman's heirs to the Los Angeles County Board of Education. I learned also that Vroman had collected Indian baskets and blankets and those collections were in the Southwest Museum, though not on display.

It was James Mink of the UCLA Library staff, who hunted down the Vroman negatives, stored in a basement of a county building; and this led to their transfer to the County Museum. There Ruth I. Mahood, curator of history, recognized the importance of the Vroman photographs, both historically and aesthetically, and prepared the volume of plates and text published by the Ward Ritchie Press as *Photographer of the Southwest.*

Charles Shelton, who succeeded Randall Henderson as publisher of *Desert Magazine,* gathered 190 historical photographs, 1860-1910, in *Photo Album of the Southwest,* with skilful annotations and in a Victorian format.

I have mentioned Laura Gilpin's book on the Rio Grande. An earlier book of hers is on *The Pueblos.* Examples of her work are found in the earliest editions of the W.P.A. New Mexico Guidebook.

Ernest Knee is another Santa Fe photographer whose work is creative. I know of only one book by him, *Santa Fe,* but what a beauty it is, capturing the ambiance of northern New Mexico, almost to the smell of piñon smoke.

In Arizona, Joseph Miller, the newspaper archivist in the Department of Library and Archives at Phoenix, is also a distinguished photographer. Several volumes of his work have been published—on Indians and on the Mission Church of San Xavier del Bac. That lovely structure, the Dove of the Desert, founded by Kino in the seventeenth century, although the present building dates from 1796, is the subject of a monograph by Ansel Adams and Nancy Newhall, in which his photographs and her text are beautifully joined; and also one by Bernard Fontana called "Biography of a Desert Church."

I have sat for hours with the crowd on the edge of the plaza at San Xavier and watched the Yaqui festival in April, the monotonous dusty dancing procession moving slowly to the obsessively repetitive music; and I have been alone to the mission on a clear winter morning, the air sweet with woodsmoke from the Papago ovens, entered the richly decorated church and paid my respects to the Blue Lady. *Faith, Fiesta, and Flowers* commemorates the blended pagan-Christian ceremony at Easter, and is another beautiful imprint from the Northland Press, with illustrations reproduced from paintings by Yaqui children.

The long file of *Arizona Highways* is a treasury of photographs in glorious color. Josef Muench is one of the most consistently successful of its photographers, and his wife Joyce has written ideal accompanying texts of pictorial trips they have made throughout Arizona. Another husband-wife team whose photographs and travel essays add to this magazine's distinction is that of Chuck Abbott and Esther Henderson.

## READING LIST

John Adair. *The Navajo and Pueblo Silversmiths.* Norman University of Oklahoma Press, 1944.

Charles Amsden. *Navajo Weaving, its Technic and History.* Santa Ana, Fine Arts Press, 1934; Albuquerque, University of New Mexico Press, 1949.

E. Boyd. *Saints and Saint Makers of New Mexico.* Santa Fe, Laboratory of Anthropology, 1946.

E. Boyd. *Popular Arts of Colonial New Mexico.* Santa Fe, Museum of International Folk Art, 1959.

Mary and Conrad Buff. *Elf Owl.* New York, Viking Press, 1958.

Raymond Carlson. *Gallery of Western Paintings.* New York, McGraw-Hill, 1951.

Van Deren Coke. *Taos and Santa Fe: The Artist's Environment, 1882-1942* Albuquerque, University of New Mexico Press, 1963.

Mildred Crews. *Patrocinio Barela.* Taos, 1962.

Ted De Grazia. *Arizona South.* No. 1, 1950—. Tucson, De Grazia Studios.

Ted De Grazia. *Padre Kino. A Portfolio depicting Memorable Events in the Life and Times of the Heroic and Immortal Priest-Colonizer.* Tucson, Arizona South, 1962.

Roland F. Dickey. *New Mexico Village Arts.* Albuquerque, University of New Mexico Press, 1949.

Frederick J. Dockstader. *Indian Art in America; the Arts and Crafts of the North American Indian.* Greenwich, Conn., New York Graphic Society, 1961.

*Faith, Flowers, and Fiestas; the Yaqui Indian Year, a Narrative of Ceremonial Events.* Tucson, University of Arizona Press, 1962.

Bernard L. Fontana. "Biography of a Desert Church; the Story of Mission San Xavier del Bac," in *The Smoke Signal,* no. 3, Spring 1961. Tucson, The Westerners, Tucson Corral.

Laura Gilpin. *The Pueblos, a Camera Chronicle.* New York, Hastings House, 1941.

Paul Horgan. " . . . Peter Hurd," in *New Mexico Magazine,* Jan. 1961, p. 8.

Paul Horgan. *The Saintmaker's Christmas Eve.* New York, Farrar, Straus, 1955.

Peter Hurd. " . . . New Mexico," in *New Mexico Magazine,* Jan. 1961, pp. 13, 36-38.

Ernest Knee. *Santa Fe, New Mexico.* New York, Hastings House, 1942.

Tom Lea. *Portfolio of Six Paintings.* Austin, University of Texas Press, 1953.

Mabel Dodge Luhan. *Taos and its Artists.* New York, Duell, Sloan, and Pearce, 1947.

Ruth I. Mahood, *ed. Photographer of the Southwest, Adam Clark Vroman, 1856-1916.* Los Angeles, The Ward Ritchie Press, 1961.

Alice Marriott. *María, The Potter of San Ildefonso.* Norman, University of Oklahoma Press, 1948.

Joseph Miller. *Arizona Indians; the People of the Sun.* New York, Hastings House, 1941.

Arthur Millier. *Maynard Dixon, Painter of the West.* Tucson, 1945.

Nancy Newhall and Ansel Adams. *Mission San Xavier del Bac.* San Francisco, 5 Associates, 1954.

Don Louis Perceval. "A Maynard Dixon Sketch Book," in *The Westerners Brand Book,* Los Angeles Corral, Book 8, 1959.

Don Louis Perceval. *A Navajo Sketch Book,* with a Descriptive Text by Clay Lockett. Flagstaff, Northland Press, 1962.

Lawrence Clark Powell. *Vroman's of Pasadena.* Pasadena, 1953.

Charles E. Shelton. *Photo Album of Yesterday's Southwest.* Palm Desert, Calif., Desert Magazine, 1961.

Eric Sloane. *Return to Taos; a Sketchbook of Roadside Americana.* New York, Funk, 1960.

Robert Taft. *Artists and Illustrators of the Old West, 1850-1900.* New York, Scribner, 1953.

Arthur Woodward. *A Brief History of Navajo Silversmithing.* (Bulletin no. 14) Flagstaff, Museum of Northern Arizona, 1938.

## viii. Books Determine

THE ACT OF LIVING is well and good, but unless one is a mystic who can break the time barrier, enter the time continuum and experience past, present, and future as one, then for the actual acts of living is he confined to the ever coming, ever going present moment. Only by reading, by what I have called the act of enchantment, can man live in the past, albeit vicariously. Only in books will he find the past usefully preserved. Without books, or their equivalents, man would lead a succession of brilliant, ephemeral moments, without the light and shade which make our recorded past.

Thus, I say, *books determine.*

Up to now I have looked at the Southwest through books about it; now let me look at books through the Southwest, to view the state of book design and printing, publishing, bookselling, collecting, reading; to visit some printers, publishers, booksellers, readers, and collectors, writers and librarians; and finally to recommend some periodicals and bibliographies which will facilitate the act of reading about the Southwest. As textbook, take *The Southwest of the Bookman,* a collection of essays on various aspects of book culture, from Lummis to Dobie.

One cannot say that books have determined the way the Southwest has developed. The explorers, missionaries, trappers, traders, stockmen and miners lived, worked and died mostly without benefit of books. Libraries came late to the Southwest. The needs and the hazards of daily life, the effect of climate and distance written about so eloquently by Patricia Paylore in *Libraries of the Southwest,* the desert dweller's over-riding need for water, beauty which blinds—these have conspired to keep book production and consumption from any considerable development in the Southwest. A map of the printers, publishers, booksellers, and libraries would be mostly wide-open space, with a few oases from El Paso to Flagstaff, Taos to Tucson.

And yet libraries and bookstores are hallmarks of civilization, are evidences of civilized society.

Wealth does not automatically create civilization and culture. Today in the Southwest, including Southern California and Texas, are many rich barbarians whose cultural life is golf, bridge, and cocktails at the country club. In all the vastness of Texas, only Austin, Dallas, and Waco support antiquarian bookshops. Phoenix, the political and economic capital of Arizona, has exactly none. If it were not for the University of Arizona, Tucson would not rate high on the Southwestern culture scale. Many rich, retired people live there and contribute nothing more than taxes. Economics determines. Good printing costs money. Someone must pay for it.

The dean of creative printers is Carl Hertzog of El Paso, who came to the region in 1923 from Pennsylvania and West Virginia, and stayed. He met Patricia Paylore's requirements for a good Southwestern bookman: he felt the pull and power of the land, he stayed, and he has left his mark. In his chapter written for *The Southwest of the Bookman,* Hertzog tells how he became a Southwestern printer. It was Maud Sullivan, city librarian of El Paso, and Tom Lea, the town's most famous native son, who "ganged up" on him and turned him into a Southwestern printer; so that in his work from about 1938, as in no other printer's, we see the color and sense the lay of the land, through his use of sandy-toned paper, illustrations by Tom Lea,

José Cisneros, and Harold Bugbee, his subjects of local history, biography, and lore; and above all, the realization of his historical position at the ancient pass site.

Individualistic and independent, a craftsman of the highest standards and integrity, Carl Hertzog is a typographical blood brother of Edwin and Robert Grabhorn of San Francisco. In California his work may be seen in depth and detail at UCLA's William Andrews Clark Memorial Library; in Texas at the University library in Austin, and the public libraries of Dallas and El Paso, in Arizona the University library in Tucson has collected his work.

University subsidization is responsible for most of the fine book printing in the Southwest. In later years Carl Hertzog has been Director of the Press at Texas Western College, a part of the statewide university. Likewise in New Mexico, the state's leading designer-publisher, Roland Dickey, is Director of the University Press in Albuquerque. He also designs and edits the *New Mexico Quarterly.* Native son of Clovis, Dickey has long used Mimbres pottery designs to give his work regional flavor; and under his direction, the University Press has printed original and classic Southwestern works.

In my bibliography of one hundred works of non-fiction on the Southwest, an after-count of their fifty-one publishers showed the University of New Mexico Press with seven titles, exceeded only by the University of Oklahoma Press with eleven. Oklahoma leads all other western university presses in quality as well as numbers; and in quality of format as well as of content. Founded by Joseph A. Brandt, who was succeeded by Savoie Lottinville, the present director, and given format of functional beauty by its long-time designer Will Ransom, the Oklahoma Press is the country's finest regional press. For their consistent excellence, its several series on Indians and on Explorations and its inexpensive Western Frontier reprints should be acquired on standing order. The Press's only weakness has been in its bibliographies, which have lacked critical editorial supervision. Rader's *South of Forty,* Campbell's *Book Lovers' Southwest,* Adams'

*Rampaging Herd,* Smith's *Travels,* are flawed by misproportion and error.

I have referred earlier to Writers' Editions, the publishing venture founded by Haniel Long in Santa Fe and which flourished in the period between the Depression and World War II. The books were designed by Walter Goodwin, Jr. and printed at the Rydal Press in Santa Fe. They have style and beauty. Writers' Editions and the Rydal Press should be written about. Some of the records for such a study are in the Haniel Long papers at the UCLA Library.

Meteoric was the New Mexican trajectory of Merle Armitage, the Los Angeles book designer, who in the 1940's and 1950's styled a few brilliant Southwest formats for publications of the Laboratory of Anthropology in Santa Fe. When he learned that the Laboratory's series of Papers in drab covers was not selling, Armitage persuaded them to let him design colorful wrappers, alive with thunderbirds and other Southwest symbols—and lo! the series sold out.

In need of study also is the history of small publishing ventures throughout the Southwest. Nearly every town and city has some kind of publishing record, which has made contributions to the mosaic of regional culture. Little is known about them. Librarians are often indifferent to what is closest to them. I have gone about the country, preaching to librarians to know and to love what is local, to be *the* authority on bookish matters in their own communities, and only then to widen out.

The most recent small press to operate in New Mexico is Jack Rittenhouse's Stagecoach Press, which has come to Santa Fe in stages via Los Angeles and Houston and which specializes in handset limited editions of books on Southwestern subjects.

In Arizona John Beecher's peripatetic Rampart Press, first of Jerome, then Scottsdale, now Phoenix, likewise had a California origin. Beecher's printing is not particularly southwestern and he favors his own poetry. The first private press in Arizona was Frank Holme's Bandar Log, out of Chicago to Ashville, North Carolina, thence to Phoenix. An account of it by Rudolf Gjelsness is in *The Southwest of the Bookman.* The largest collection of Holme and his work, including books and original drawings, is in the University of Arizona Library at Tucson.

Dale Stuart King of Six Shooter Canyon, Globe, is Arizona's leading publisher of regional works of natural history and archaeology.

In recent years the University of Arizona Press has sought to close the gap between it and the university presses of Oklahoma and New Mexico; and under the direction of Jack L. Cross, it has made efforts at good design and format.

Another Tucson publishing house, Arizona Silhouettes, founded by George W. Chambers, has laudably issued valuable Arizoniana, including the reprint of *Vanished Arizona,* annotated by Ray Brandes, but the format of these works is crude and unattractive.

In contrast is the serene format achieved by the Arizona Pioneers' Historical Society of Tucson in its publications on the W. J. Holliday Fund, designed and printed one and all by Lawton Kennedy of San Francisco.

Neither Tucson nor Phoenix, the state's largest cities, has matched the record of Flagstaff, that little railroad and lumbering town up in Coconino County. To it came two "barbarians" from beyond the River, Paul A. Weaver, Jr., publisher-printer from Pacific Palisades, followed by John Anderson, designer from Los Angeles. Weaver acquired a small printing shop, re-named it the Northland Press, and proceeded forthwith to produce the most beautiful books ever made in Arizona. Heralded by Donald M. Powell's *An Arizona Fifty,* a model bibliography issued in 1962 to commemorate Arizona's 50th anniversary of statehood, *A Navajo Sketch Book* and *Torrent in the Desert* are at the peak of fine book work in the Southwest.

In Los Angeles the Ward Ritchie Press and Paul Bailey's Westernlore Press, the Huntington Library, and Glen Dawson have published distinguished Southwestern books.

Printshops and publishers' offices are busy places that do not welcome socializing visitors. Private collectors guard their privacy. Libraries are places for quiet reading and study.

So where can a man go who wants to talk about the Southwest with people who share his interest? *The Westerners* is one answer—regional groups around the country, and as far away as New York, Washington, and London, that meet at dinner to hear papers on Western themes. Most of them publish periodicals. *The Westerners,* however, are for men only, for honest-to-cactus, creosote-blooded he-men.

Where are women to go? Or married people? To bookshops—those open places where one can browse or buy, can talk or listen, often drink coffee or stronger "on the house;" and if one feels "time's winged chariot hovering near," knows that it is in idling gear. Large new bookshops throughout the country are not what I mean, although they will stock the recently published and the standard series on the Southwest, including the many paperbacks. Dawson's Book Shop in Los Angeles is the best place in that city to find current ephemera on the Southwest—pamphlets, periodicals, privately printed opuscula, etc. Their catalogs should be read by those who wish to acquire current and older items. Glen Dawson is knowledgeable, not only of books but of the land. He and his brother Muir are mountain-climbers.

My fondest preference is for smaller shops, often one-man, or one-woman, or one-couple shops, sometimes in private quarters, where individualism is enshrined. Beyond the Southwest, there is Zoe and Wright Howes' apartment-shop in Chicago, where one finds sanctuary in winter, snug by the grate, Siamese cats climbing the drapes, old Wrightie with glass in hand, discoursing on a lifetime of collecting for such great bookmen as Everett Graff, E. De Golyer, and Thomas W. Streeter. Or Rosalie and Jack Reynolds' shop in the San Fernando Valley, one of the most knowledgeable and hospitable of all Southwest couples. Reynolds' catalogues are outstanding, often with prefaces by Southwestern writers. To *The Southwest of the Bookman* Reynolds contributed a searching chapter called "The Making of a Southwestern Bookseller." Yale and Brown of Pasadena have the lighthearted, friendly manner, overlying a sound knowledge of Southern Californiana.

There is also Los Artesanos, on the plaza in Old Las Vegas (and I don't mean Nevada), the high-ceilinged book and art shop of Diana and Joe Stein, featuring Southwestern books and local crafts, a cultural oasis in a town that is still frontier. It is not limited to regional material. I found there a salt-and-pepper set in Danish teak, and a run of Haydns and Mozarts in the Penguin scores series.

On my way to Los Artesanos one time, after a visit to the campus of New Mexico Highlands University in New Town, I was swept up by an ecclesiastical procession and carried along past the shop and on up the Gallinas to Montezuma, the old Santa Fe Railroad hotel and spa, now a Jesuit seminary for Mexican students. The seminary's twenty-fifth anniversary was being consecrated by the Bishop of Durango and other colorful clerics. A couple of hours passed before I made my way back downstream to the bookshop.

The Taos Bookshop is a similar haven where one can find sanctuary from tourist traffic that clogs the town in summer. In the *Southwest Review* are two beautiful essays by Claire Morrill, the shop's owner, which tell about its place in the life of the community.

In his *Rodgers Library Notes,* William S. Wallace, Librarian of New Mexico Highlands University, has published accounts of this and other Southwestern bookshops, written by their owners, an example of the way the region's bookmen can draw together in a common cultural front.

Nancy Lane's Villagrá Bookshop near the Palace of the Governors in Santa Fe and the neighboring Ancient City Bookshop are places of rendezvous for the booklover, as is Old Town Books on the Plaza, Fair Plaza Bookshop, and the New Mexico Book Co. store, all in Albuquerque; and farther down river, Mesilla Book and Art

Center has Carl Hertzog imprints on the shelves and Peter Hurd paintings on the wall, as well as the warmest of welcomes. Clark Wright of El Paso is also a good source for Hertzogiana and other Southwestern Americana.

From Mesilla over the Continental Divide and down the Gila is a long dry march before the next oasis is reached, the Overland Bookshop of Dorothy McNamee, her shop-in-home on the north side of Tucson. Here this lucky wanderer was served rare beef and rare books by candle-light, and warmed by friendship. And then one can go on marching all over the state of Arizona and not find such another bookshop. The cultural differences between Arizona and New Mexico that we have noted throughout this book are illustrated in this imbalance of intimate bookshops.

In modern times the great private book collectors have not enriched the libraries of New Mexico and Arizona. H. H. Bancroft's collections were sold to the University of California at Berkeley. Dr. Joseph A. Munk's collection of Arizoniana, offered originally to the University of Arizona upon condition of it providing fire-proof housing for it, went by default to the Southwest Museum in Los Angeles. Henry E. Huntington's librarians have long combed the Southwest to send material west to San Marino. The Edward Ayer collection on the American Indian and the West, inspired by young Lieutenant Ayer's reading while stationed on the Arizona frontier near Arivaca, is in the Newberry Library at Chicago, to which institution Everett Graff is giving his even greater collection of Western Americana. Thomas W. Streeter's peerless Texas collection was sold to Yale, which also received as a gift the vast Coe collection on the West, with an endowment to enlarge, edit, and publish its treasures. An exception is the late E. de Golyer's collection which has been founded in trust at Southern Methodist University in Dallas.

The W. J. Holliday collection of Western Americana, rich in Arizoniana, was dispersed at auction in 1954. I was in New York at the time of this sale and rejoiced to see some of the choicest pieces go back where they came from, when they were acquired by the University of Arizona Library. Exceptional also is T. E. Hanley of Bradford, Pennsylvania, who has given the University of Arizona Library nearly 50,000 volumes, though not Southwestern in subject.

Senators Barry Goldwater and Clinton Anderson of Arizona and New Mexico respectively, are Southwestern bookmen, and the former is a photographer who has specialized in recording historic sites in Arizona.

In both states there is a renaissance of interest in history. The University libraries in Tucson, Tempe, and Albuquerque have made provisions for special collections. The University of Arizona has a historian-collector in the field, following the lead of the Huntington, the Bancroft, and the UCLA libraries. In Tucson the University and the Pioneers' Society sponsor an annual conference on Arizona history. There is concern in New Mexico and Arizona over the destruction of historical landmarks. Fort Union near Las Vegas and Fort Lowell in Tucson are being restored.

Until Arizona's Udall became Secretary of the Interior in the Kennedy cabinet, Southwestern politicians were not outspoken on behalf of history and conservation. President Theodore Roosevelt was the last of the great western spokesmen. The times call for another such champion if the natural colors of the land are not to be lost in a blaze of neon, views blotted out by billboards, old plazas ripped apart by freeways, and the earth itself black-topped to death.

A SOUTHWESTERN READER, wherever he may be, cannot spend all of his time in the field, combing the bookshops for current and classic Southwestern items. How then does he keep up with the literature and extend his reading backward in time? Lifelong reading is called for. Periodicals and bibliographies are the guides, are the tools.

There is no single periodical which covers the entire field of current publishing in the Southwest today. The closest to this is the monthly checklist *Books of the Southwest,* issued since 1957 by the

UCLA School of Library Service and edited by Betty Rosenberg and myself. Our effort is to include ephemeral as well as standard items, many free for the asking; and Miss Rosenberg compiles occasional fiction and juvenile supplements. The area includes Southern California, as well as Arizona, New Mexico, Western Texas, and Oklahoma.

Occasionally from 1934 to 1946 and monthly since then, I have contributed a book page called "Western Books and Writers" to *Westways,* the magazine of the Automobile Club of Southern California, in which I feature the regional rather than the national.

The best bibliographical source on current Arizoniana, including official publications, is the checklist by Donald M. Powell in the *Arizona Quarterly*. There is no comparable source for New Mexico, although the *New Mexico Quarterly* and the *New Mexico Magazine* carry reviews and listings of selected publications.

The quarterly *Arizona and the West* at the University of Arizona; *Arizoniana,* the periodical of the Arizona Pioneers' Historical Society; *Smoke Signal,* issued by the Tucson Corral of the Westerners and *The Round-Up,* a similar publication of the Los Angeles Corral; *The Master Key,* the quarterly of the Southwest Museum; the monthly *Desert Magazine;* the *Southern California Quarterly;* the *New Mexico Historical Review; El Palacio* (Museum of New Mexico); *The Kiva* (Arizona State Museum); *The Plateau* (Museum of Northern Arizona) all carry reviews and notices.

The best literary periodical of the region is the *Southwest Review,* edited by Allen Maxwell and Margaret L. Hartley, and published by the Southern Methodist University Press in Dallas. Throughout the half century of its life, J. Frank Dobie has been a constant contributor. Mrs. Hartley writes wisely of current books in "Southwestern Chronicle." The *Texas Quarterly* does not include book reviews.

What bibliographies are essential? Note the plural; there is no single bibliography that covers or says it all. The closest anyone has come to it is a compilation by Mary Tucker called *Books of the Southwest, a General Bibliography,* a handy paperback of 105 pages, published in 1937 and thus a quarter century out of date. The arrangement is classified, with some annotations and includes the Indian, Spanish, and American periods, and sections on Natural Sciences, Travel and Description, and Literature, including fiction, poetry, and children's books.

This seems to have been the only book by Mary Tucker. I located her, living in Colorado Springs, and learned that she had originally been associated with Erna Fergusson and Fred Harvey. Let her tell it:

"As one of the couriers on the guided tours which Erna Fergusson organized for the railroad, with headquarters in Santa Fe, I came to know many books of the Southwest and found that our visitors were very much interested in them too. We were most fortunate in having Miss Fergusson, Kenneth Chapman, Harry Mera, many of the artists, and others, on our original 'faculty'. It was a distinguished introduction to the country, which we all came to love.

"Compiling the reading list was an entirely personal project, which I began with considerably more optimism than at the end, and had it not been a labor of love as well would have closed the book. I had no bibliographical training at all and should have gone back to college at that point and started over again. Most of the checking was done in the New York Public Library, since I was in the east at that time."

Henry R. Wagner's *The Spanish Southwest* and *The Plains and the Rockies* are the classic bibliographies of the older periods. Thomas W. Streeter's monumental *Bibliography of Texas* is in the Wagner tradition.

The best bibliography on New Mexico is Lyle Saunder's *Guide to Materials Bearing on Cultural Relations in New Mexico.* There is nothing comparable on Arizona. Donald M. Powell's *An Arizona*

*Gathering* and *An Arizona Fifty,* point toward the larger bibliography he intends to compile. Francis P. Farquhar's *Books of the Colorado River and the Grand Canyon* is the best river bibliography. *Desert Voices* by E. I. Edwards is a profusely annotated bibliography of the Mojave and Colorado deserts. Ramon F. Adams' *Six Guns and Saddle Leather* lists bad-men literature, and his *The Rampaging Herd* is a bibliography of the cattle industry. J. C. Dykes' *Billy the Kid; the Bibliography of a Legend* is a model work on a single person. Mildred Harrington's *The Southwest in Children's Books* is unique.

My criticism of bibliographers is that too often they include books they have not personally evaluated; and in my own work I have described only books that I have read, thought about, and lived with for a time. *Land of Fiction* and *Heart of the Southwest* are my selections of the best novels and stories about Southern California and the Southwest; to a new edition of *Libros Californianos* by Phil Townsend Hanna I added what I regarded as the best works on California published between 1932 and 1957; and in *A Southwestern Century* I selected one hundred outstanding works of non-fiction. All of my bibliographies are annotated. The making of unannotated book lists is work for machines, not men.

This brings us back full circle to the most humane of all reading lists on the region, Dobie's *Guide to Life and Literature of the Southwest.* If you must jettison all other books in your baggage, keep Dobie for ballast.

Lastly, some words about the outstanding library collections on the Southwest—non-circulating reference libraries where one may go and expect to find the books there, ready to be used. There aren't many of them, and the best are not even in the Southwest. Yale's Coe Collection, under the curatorship of Archibald Hanna, and the Ayer-Graff collections in Chicago's Newberry Library, whose curator is Colton Storm, are among the finest in their extent, housing, and provisions for use.

In California the Bancroft Library at the University of California in Berkeley is the most famous of all collections of manuscript and archival materials on the West. Its treasures have never been fully catalogued, nor has it ever been given housing equal to its importance. In Southern California the Huntington Library and the Southwest Museum are the two best libraries on our chosen region. UCLA's Special Collections is strong in Southern Californiana.

In Arizona the Department of Library and Archives in the State Capitol at Phoenix is strongest on early newspapers. Neither it nor the Arizona State University Library at Tempe has made adequate provision for the care and use of their Arizoniana, although the latter library plans to do so in a new building. In Tucson the University of Arizona Library has established a Department of Special Collections for the collection, care, and use of Arizoniana, printed and manuscript; and across the street at the Arizona Pioneers' Historical Society good work is being done to collect and preserve Arizona source materials and pioneers' artifacts. The Museum of Northern Arizona at Flagstaff has a model small reference library on the region. Some kind of cooperative program would benefit these now competitive Arizona libraries.

New Mexico's complex of state supported museums, historical societies, and state library extension service is confusing, and has not resulted in a single major reference library the state's ancient culture calls for.

The University of New Mexico in Albuquerque is the only one of the universities and colleges that has made adequate provision for its research and reference materials on the Southwest. In the University Library's Coronado Room such a facility exists, although in funds for collecting it is inadequately supported. New Mexico's libraries also would benefit from a cooperative collecting program. Neither Arizona nor New Mexico can look to California for inspiration.

In El Paso the Public Library gained fame in the regime of Librarian Maud Sullivan for its Southwest Room; and under Helen Farrington it acquired a new building with murals by Tom Lea. Lea's tribute to Mrs. Sullivan was printed by Carl Hertzog for graduates of the UCLA Library School; he concluded:

"In 1908 Maud Durlin left the familiar green valleys of her native Wisconsin and came to West Texas, to live by the dusty edge of the Rio Bravo del Norte and became the librarian of El Paso's Public Library.

"When she died thirty-five years later, by the same Rio Bravo and still El Paso's librarian, she had made with her mind and energy one of the richest contributions a good citizen ever brought to West Texas. It was a gift imponderable and impossible accurately to measure and survey, for in its most important aspect it was entirely a thing of the spirit: a force working to enlarge civilization, a gift offered to the mind. Both her life and her library were devoted to the offering of this gift. When she died, this had become not only her contribution but her reward."

"In the arid Southwest," wrote Patricia Paylore, in words which surely apply to Maud Sullivan, "it takes more to be a good librarian than elsewhere. An ordinary man just won't do."

## READING LIST

Ramon F. Adams. *The Rampaging Herd.* Norman, University of Oklahoma Press, 1959.

Ramon F. Adams. *Six-Guns & Saddle Leather; a Bibliography of Books and Pamphlets on Western Outlaws and Gunmen.* Norman, University of Oklahoma Press, 1954.

Walter S. Campbell (Stanley Vestal). *The Book Lover's Southwest: a Guide to Good Reading.* Norman, University of Oklahoma Press, 1955.

Edwin Castagna. "Public Libraries in the Southwest," in *Libraries in the Southwest.*

Jefferson C. Dykes. *Billy the Kid, the Bibliography of a Legend.* Albuquerque, University of New Mexico Press, 1952.

E. I. Edwards. *Desert Voices, a Descriptive Bibliography.* Los Angeles, Westernlore Press, 1961.

Francis P. Farquhar. *The Books of the Colorado River and the Grand Canyon: a Selective Bibliography.* (Early California Travels Series, 12) Los Angeles, Glen Dawson, 1953.

Rudolph H. Gjelsness. "Frank Holme: Newspaper Artist and Designer of Books," in *The Southwest of the Bookman.*

Phil Townsend Hanna. *Libros Californianos: or, Five Feet of California Books.* Rev. and enl. by Lawrence Clark Powell. Los Angeles, Zeitlin and Ver Brugge, 1958.

Mildred P. Harrington. *The Southwest in Children's Books, a Bibliography.* Baton Rouge, Louisiana State University Press, 1952.

Carl Hertzog. "The Printer at the Pass," in *The Southwest of the Bookman.*

William J. Holliday. *Western Americana, many of great rarity; the distinguished collection formed by William J. Holliday . . . sold by his order, April 20-22, 1954.* New York, Parke-Bernet Galleries, 1954.

Tom Lea. *Maud Durlin Sullivan.* Los Angeles, University of California School of Library Service, 1962.

Claire Morrill. "The Indispensable Bookman," and "The Pinon Smoke of Taos," in *Southwest Review,* Summer 1962, pp. 238-243; Autumn 1962, pp. 319-322.

Patricia Paylore. "The Effect of Climate and Distance on Libraries in the Arid Regions," in *Libraries in the Southwest.*

Donald M. Powell. *Arizona Fifty, a List of Fifty Books About Arizona Published Since Statehood.* Tucson, Arizona Pioneers' Historical Society, 1962.

Donald M. Powell. *An Arizona Gathering. A Bibliography of Arizoniana, 1950-1959.* Tucson, Arizona Pioneers' Historical Society, 1960.

Lawrence Clark Powell. *Act of Enchantment; an address . . .* Historical Society of New Mexico, 1960. Houston, Stagecoach Press, 1961.

Lawrence Clark Powell. *Heart of the Southwest: a Selective Bibliography of Novels, Stories, and Tales Laid in Arizona and New Mexico and Adjacent Lands.* Los Angeles, Printed for Dawson's Book Shop at the Plantin Press, 1955.

Lawrence Clark Powell. *Land of Fiction. Thirty-two Novels and Stories about Southern California, from Ramona to The Loved One. A Bibliographical Essay.* Los Angeles, Glen Dawson, 1952.

Lawrence Clark Powell, *ed. Libraries in the Southwest:* Their Growth, Strengths, Needs, in Papers presented by a Conference of Librarians and

Writers co-sponsored by the Rockefeller Foundation, Occidental College, and the California Library Association, and held at Occidental College, April 16, 1955. (Occasional Paper no. 3) Los Angeles, University of California Library, 1955.

Lawrence Clark Powell. *The Roots of Regional Literature.* Las Vegas, New Mexico, Rodgers Library, 1959.

Lawrence Clark Powell, *ed. The Southwest of the Bookman, Essays from Various Sources,* collected by Lawrence Clark Powell. (Occasional Paper no. 11) Los Angeles, University of California Library, 1959.

Lawrence Clark Powell. *A Southwestern Century. A Bibliography of One Hundred Books of Non-Fiction about the Southwest.* Van Nuys, Calif., J. E. Reynolds, 1958.

Jesse Rader. *South of Forty, from the Mississippi to the Rio Grande, a Bibliography.* Norman, University of Oklahoma Press, 1947.

Lyle Saunders. *A Guide to Materials Bearing on Cultural Relations in New Mexico,* Albuquerque, University of New Mexico Press, 1944.

Thomas W. Streeter. *Bibliography of Texas, 1795-1845.* 3 parts in 5 vols. Cambridge, Harvard University Press, 1955-1960.

Mary Tucker. *Books of the Southwest, A General Bibliography.* New York, J. J. Augustin, 1937.

Henry R. Wagner. *The Spanish Southwest, 1542-1794; an Annotated Bibliography.* 2 vols. Albuquerque, The Quivira Society, 1937.

## Epilogue

IF I AM OBSESSED by the flow of water, and by the lack of it in Southwestern rivers, so am I also haunted by mountains, those upthrusts of landscape which keep the region from being monotonous. Because of the clear air, one never loses sight of mountains in the Southwest, even though they be a hundred miles away.

From Mt. Wheeler to triple-peaked Truchas, from Mt. Taylor to Shiprock, and from Bill Williams Mountain to the San Francisco peaks at Flagstaff, one's vision is relayed by mountains clear across the landscape of northern New Mexico and Arizona. "Turn whichever way we might," wrote Martha Summerhayes of Bill Williams, "still this purple mountain was before us."

In southern Arizona I was once held in similar thrall by Mount Graham, highest peak of the Pinaleno range. Starting in the morning from the shelter of the Catalinas down in Pima County and following the San Pedro to the Gila, the Gila to San Carlos, I swung around the magnetic pole of Graham, great blue-shouldered, white-capped, cloud-crowned mountain, obviously an abode of the gods; and by afternoon I had left Safford at the mountain's northern base, headed south toward the snowy Dos Cabezas, glimpsed the distant Chiricahuas (the Cheery Cows), then ran due west through a symphony of musical ranges: the Dragoons and the Little Dragoons, the

Giliuros, Huachucas, Whetstones and the Santa Ritas, finally reaching Tucson's guardian Rincons and Catalinas—a five-hundred-mile day, watched over all the way, safeguarded by those sacred mountains of the Southwest.

On Kitt Peak west-southwest of Tucson, I have admired the solar telescope and other marvels, but what I coveted was the firewood rights retained by the Papagos, as I saw windfalls of oak for the gathering, that sweet-smoked, slow-burning best of all woods, a whole mountainside of it. Farther west, Baboquívari, sacred peak of the Papagos, stood still inviolate, thankfully too steep for skiing and other indignities.

The mountains of the Southwest are sacred to all who cherish wilderness, be they Indian, Spanish, or Anglo. They will be the last parts of the landscape to fall to progress, safe in our time from the bulldozer, the billboard, the ballyhoo. You who take to the road to see a Southwest you have read about, or take to books to read about a Southwest you have seen, lift up your eyes to these mountains and speak the litany of their names. It is they who bring down water from the sky to make rivers, which in turn have given the Southwest its ancient cultures, in the great chain of life, of which man is only one link.

And thus the last words should be *mountains determine.*

# Index